Rabbis in Love

Personal Stories

Marilyn Bronstein and Philip Alan Belove

LoveWise Press
Saint Johnsbury, VT

Available from www.rabbis-in-love.com,
Amazon.com, CreateSpace.com,
on Kindle and other retail outlets

Copyright by LoveWise Press
Philip Alan Belove and Marilyn Bronstein
All rights reserved

Copyright April, 2012
Copyright Registration: TXu 1-802=877

ISBN 978-0-9854036-0-7

Advance Acclaim

Gives you a soulful glimpse of realistic and spiritually romantic ways for couples to relate. It is a warmhearted and inspiring read. – **Rabbi Zalman Schachter-Shalomi,** author of Davening (Jewish Lights)

As Rumi says, "Lovers don't finally meet somewhere. They're in each other all along." The love stories in this book have been with us all along, yet the authors have now done the mitzvah of allowing us to join the couples they interviewed on the journey of the heart to which we all belong. **Cedric Speyer**, M.A., M.Ed., Clinical Supervisor of E-Counseling; Creative Director of InnerView Guidance International.

"I love this book! In strikingly non-interventional interviews, the authors have drawn from their participating rabbinic couples emotionally uninhibited and yet delicately modest dialogues that offer us all profoundly magical, cross-culturally relevant, true stories about the beauty possible between two people, committed to each other in every way over time. It is a warm invitation, calling out to us, 'Come on in here and hear about love!'" – **Ani Meharry,** Ph.D. in Psychology, author of Fourth Dimensional Relating: A New Frontier for the Couple.

"I found the reading of this to be an unexpected and profoundly moving experience. I am weeping openly as I write; this little collection has re-awakened a profound yearning......something so primal, so deep, that it is hard to understand how it came to be buried." – **V.C.,** Duxbury, MA.

"Excellent, very well conceived and written, compelling, encourages and engages the reader." – **Julian Cohen,** Business and Personal Development Coach

Table of Contents

Acknowledgements

Introduction:
This is a Book about Love   1

Chapter One:
**The Wings of Love
and the Sheltered Nest of the Sabbath**   8

Chapter Two:
This Love, Like the Moon in All Its Phases
Rabbi Leibish and Deena Hundert   32

Chapter Three:
Without Touching, Without Gazing, No Intimate Exchange of Words For Seven Years, and Yet...
Rabbi Yisroel & Sara Bernath   52

Chapter Four:
How Different Can Two Be and Still Be One?
Rabbi Haim & Caroline Sherrf   76

Chapter Five:
Do Not Awaken Love Until it is Ripe
Rabbi Shefa Gold & Rachmiel O'Regan   100

Looking for Lilith
Rabbi Ohad & Dawn Cherie Ezrahi   124

Chapter Seven
Two Rabbis, One Soul
Rabbi Victor Gross & Rabbi Nadya Gross   168

Chapter Eight
Being There
Rabbi Laura and Charles Kaplan   190

Chapter Nine
All the Waters of the Flood Cannot Drown Love
Rabbi Lisa Grushcow & Rabbi Andrea Myers   214

Afterword   250

So, From Under the Bed, What Did I Learn?
Philip Alan Belove   251

Under the Bed, What Did I Learn?
Marilyn Bronstein   264

Epilogue   278

About these interviews
We were working with spoken material and translating it to written material. We have tried to be as true as possible to the actual voices of the people who so generously contributed their stories. Some of these folks are using English as a second language. Many have very idiosyncratic rhythms, quite charming, and we've tried to preserve this. Nonetheless, we have made some minor changes and edited what they have said only when necessary for the sake of clarity and brevity.

Acknowledgements
So many people to thank for this. First of all, I want to thank my collaborator, Marilyn Bronstein. This would not have happened without her. Second, I want to thank the Rabbi couples who so generously shared their wisdom and some of their secrets with us. Also, I want to thank my many friends in Montreal. Montreal is a city which is culturally rich and spiritually generous and I believe much of what has blossomed in me during the creation of this book was due to all the time I spent there and the many friends I made. Beyond that I want to thank my mother and father, Rose and Leonard Belove. The mysteries and strengths of their love for each other led me into this project and through it. I want to thank my dear friend, Gwendalin Kohler, for her wise advice, support and challenges. Beyond that, I am continually grateful to my old teachers, Robert L. Powers, Jack Wideman, Joseph Campbell, and Gregory Bateson, for the help they gave me in framing my own vision. And finally, and I'm not sure how to put this, but this work is the result of a calling and that in itself seems to be a bit of a miracle. I wish to acknowledge and praise the Source of that calling. -- Philip Alan Belove

Thank you to all the Rabbis that I have known who have inspired me and shared their wisdom with me. Thank you to all the people who have taught me what love is: my grandparents, my parents, my children, my siblings. Thank you to David, my beloved (that's what the name means) who has truly taught me what it means to love with all your heart and soul. Thank you to all my friends who helped proof-read, who gave advice and listened while I blabbed on about my project. Thank you to all the people who I have collaborated with in the past, Terry, Yehudit, Helga, Diana, Vera. You have all contributed to preparing me for this "extreme collaboration" I have been involved in the past three years. Most important, thank you to my collaborator, Philip who was not afraid to wrestle me to the ground, metaphorically, as we chiseled out each other's personalities. – Marilyn Bronstein

Introduction

"There is only One Story and it's your Love Story,"
Rabbi Ronnie Cahana.

This is a book about love.

It's about what love looks like in real life, and also about what love can look like when it's a spiritual practice.

This is a book of stories from couples who are very much in love and at least one of the partners is a Rabbi. Of course, you don't have to be Jewish to learn something from how a Rabbi and spouse make their love-nest. Every cultural group likes to think, "We're unique." Our claim is that we're just like everyone else, only more so.

Rabbis aren't monks. They fall in love, they marry, they have families. It's expected. Jewish spirituality is rooted in daily family life; the joy, the passion, the tears, "the whole enchilada", or as Jews would say, the whole *megilla*.

If you are one of those folks who take pleasure in getting a little *ferclempt*, which is Yiddish for "choked up about something nice," you will probably enjoy reading these stories. There is something in Jewish culture that says it's a good thing to feel deeply.

We did not create this to be a how-to book, although we do think it contains inspiring lessons. *Rabbis in Love* is first of all a book of stories.

If you're a busy executive type and can't wait to know the bottom line, the "Secrets-to-True-Love-that-Rabbis-Know," skip ahead to the last chapter. But then come back and read the interviews. Hearing someone's stories about how they live their love is so much richer than merely hearing homilies.

A Relationship is a Story in Two Voices

Stories are a great way to capture relationships because stories tell you about what he did and then what she did and then what he did, round and round.

It's especially interesting to hear from both partners. You get to see how they are with each other, how they embellish and correct each other.

That is why we've kept the dialogue between the couples intact. It wasn't an easy decision. The synthesized voice is very tidy; the voice of dialogue has all these interesting loose ends and you get more of a feeling for the relationship.

And then there is us.

As we assembled this book, we started to realize that it was also the story of how our own relationship evolved. For three years we interviewed together, edited together, discussed, argued, disagreed and synthesized. Through this process our relationship changed and we changed.

You might be able to get a sense of this as you read the progression of commentaries we wrote together after each interview. At first, we wrote our commentaries in one voice. But after a while that seemed inadequate. We really did have differing perspectives and so we ourselves had to start appearing in dialogue.

So, here is a peek into how we began. In two voices. So you can get a sense of our relationship. We'll start by each describing the moment we first realized we were going to do something important together, the Genesis Moment, as we call it. Every relationship has one.

Philip: The memory I hold is of the time we were sitting in this restaurant eating chicken soup (actually Vietnamese pho) and comparing notes on our Jewish backgrounds and philosophies. You suggested we collaborate on something. I said, "Well, the strangest idea I ever had was about 25 years ago in graduate school. It occurred to me that the next Messiah will be a couple." And you said, "That's funny. I had the same idea almost 35 years ago."

Marilyn: In my mind the story begins even earlier when you showed me a book you were working on. I remember just jumping in and starting to edit. It was obvious to me even then that we had collaboration chemistry. But then I do remember the conversation about the Messiah in the restaurant.

It was maybe a week later. I remember saying, for me, this *Moshiach* couple would be a model of what a great loving relationship could be. Like, "Okay, you think you're the *Moshiach*? If you're so enlightened, let me see how you live with someone. That's the true test of your spirituality.

And, by the way, let's hear what your partner has to say about that."

Philip: Did you notice that twice you remembered having realizations before I did? First, it was about the collaboration and then it was your 10 year lead on the Messiah idea? I've had to think about that.

Marilyn: So we decided to collaborate on this *Moshiach* idea we shared. We would talk to couples committed to a spiritual path, and also committed to each other. Where would we find such people?

Philip: Since we're both Jewish, it was obvious. We would interview Rabbis and their partners. We'd do a book called "Rabbis in Love." Loved the title.

Marilyn: And then it was a year into the project and I realized that we were talking about two totally different visions of a *Moshiach* couple.

Philip: Yes, my idea of Messiah was quite different. It took a while to see where we differed. I'm slower to speak up sometimes. We've had to learn how to adjust to each other's rhythms.

For me, each loving relationship becomes the Messiah for the partners, their spiritual teacher. A Love Relationship changes who you are.

Each relationship really does have a mind of its own. It challenges the partners. It encourages them to stay open to learning. There are always things they can learn in order to love better.

It's only sometimes that relationships work as a unity. The differences are important. That's a very couple-as-Messiah realization. As we've worked together, we've learned to appreciate how we differ and how our differences are a resource.

Marilyn: They are a resource but they are also a challenge.

We bring very different sensibilities to the project. I tend to get into the Jewish stuff. I've always been fascinated with the love stories in the Bible. I love the way they tell us about relationships that are not perfect.

But the way they related then is not so relevant to my life today. I'm looking for new models for love. This project really is my personal quest to find loving couples who can share a spiritual vision, passionately disagree, and yet still live together. I'm looking for my *Moshiach* couples.

Philip: I never imagined I'd find Jewish studies so congenial. If you've been fascinated by the love stories in the Bible, I have been fascinated by the love stories people tell about their own relationships.

I was always deeply fascinated by love. My family name really is Belove, and I was teased for it in high school. *Be Love.* But in later life I've come to think that maybe my name has been my calling.

I hold a doctorate in counseling psychology. I do a blog at drbelove.com. I have worked with couples and relationship issues for years. So much exposure to how love could go wrong. I wanted to learn more about the many different ways love can go right.

Marilyn: And here we are, trying to create one book, with one voice.

Philip: While we may have separate sensibilities, we do share a vision.

Falling in Love is a Spiritual Awakening

The task of lovers in a spiritual partnership is to prove to each other that their union is more than only flesh, that their life together matters. How they live and love each other matters deeply. And not only to them, but also to all the lives they touch.

For us, the classic phrase, "and they lived happily ever after", closes the door on the most interesting part of the story. If one is looking for wisdom, then, finally getting together is not the end of the story. It's the beginning. We wanted to hear what happened after they got together.

The Blue Thread

We asked folks for stories about what loving and living together had taught them.

After each interview we share what struck us about this particular couple, in a section we call "the blue thread." Why "blue thread"? When a Jewish couple is married, they stand under the *tallis* (prayer shawl) and it becomes a *chuppah*, a canopy, to sanctify their union, and every *tallis*, every *chuppah*, has at least one blue thread as a reminder of The Divine.

With each couple, we wanted to know what were the divine threads, the themes of love that bound this couple together?"

Why is this relationship different from all other relationships?

To understand what is unique about each couple we asked them four questions; the *Mah Nishtanah:*

> What was the Genesis moment, the moment when you first realized that this relationship was going to be significant?
>
> How does the relationship currently challenge you?
>
> How did you change as result of being in this relationship?
>
> How does your relationship influence your understanding of Judaism, and vice-versa?

As in the Passover Seder, we asked that the questions be answered with stories, no theories.

We spoke to male Rabbis, female Rabbis, Rabbis married to each other, Rabbis who were converts, Rabbis of differing sexual orientations. All the couples we interviewed practiced Judaism in very different ways. We spoke to Orthodox Rabbis, Renewal, Conservative, Reform, and, probably most esoteric, followers of the Hebraic Path. Quite a spectrum.

Each couple found their own unique way of interweaving their love with their Jewish Spirituality. One couple used the lovers in the Song of Songs as their inspiration. Another used the relationship between Lilith and Adam at the very beginning of the human story in Genesis as theirs. Many spoke about how observing the Sabbath each week deepened their intimacy.

Spirituality was also very much in the bedroom. One couple said that it was not until their wedding day that they even touched each other's hand. Another spoke about the physical experience of making love as a way to experience the presence of God. Another couple described the "kissing meditation" they performed on their first date. One couple happily referred to the teaching in the Talmud which says that it is the obligation of a man to please his wife in making love.

And Speaking of the Talmud and the Bedroom, One More Story.

We were at the dining room table with Rabbi Leibish and his wife, Deena. Deena said, "Why don't you tell Philip and Marilyn the story you told your class yesterday."

Leibish said, "There is a story in the Talmud; one of the most prominent Rabbis of the Talmud. He's known as just *Rav*, "The Rabbi." One of his students, Rabbi Kahana, wanted to see how Rav would act during marital intimacy with his wife. So the student hid under the bed of his teacher, Rav.

"So when Rav, who was an austere, holy person, came into the room to be with his wife, he was laughing, being very passionate and expressive in his love, and very emotional. And his student was so taken aback that after a while he yelled out, 'The mouth of my Rebbe seems like the mouth of someone who has not eaten for a long time!'

"And Rav said, '*Ahd k'day Kach!* This is too much!' Like: 'Kahana What in God's name are you doing here?'

And Kahana, says, "This is also Torah I need to learn."

As Reb Leibish pointed out, "The Talmud teaching is that the ideal is to be passionate, to be loving, to be expressive. There's a tendency to think that passion and expression of love is something that holy people don't do. By telling it as a story, specifically of a prominent Rabbi, we understand."

We need stories about real people. In this book we are following this ancient tradition.

We are approaching sacred ground.

When this Talmud story was told, people lived in close communities with little privacy. It was easy to see a couple walking down the street or hear an argument from the kitchen. Today, however, we each live in separated worlds.

Ordinarily when people talk about their intimate relationships, they do it from a distance. They talk about principles and lessons learned. They don't share what actually happened. In sharing these stories with us, the couples we've interviewed have sacrificed some of their privacy because they know "this is Torah we all need to learn." We have to be grateful and respectful. We must remove our shoes. We are about to enter sacred ground.

So please, join us under the bed.

Chapter One

The Wings of Love and The Sheltered Nest of The Sabbath

Rabbi Ronnie and Karen Cahana

To be known just as we are; I think that's what's built into Shabbat, into the system of Shabbat. This is a time of eternal paradise. And it's just strolling together because 'that's the only person I want to be with.' I can't wait for that. Every Shabbat we bless each other. Every Shabbat we tell each other our secrets – Rabbi Ronnie

This [gesturing between her and Ronnie] is Home. It doesn't really matter where we are. But wherever we are together, this is Home. - Karen

Marc Chagal, a Jewish artist in the first half of the 20th century, painted pictures of sleepy Jewish towns in Old Eastern Europe. There were fiddlers on roofs, giant birds and lovers floating in the magic of a kiss. For us, this interview with Ronnie and Karen was like wandering through a Chagal painting.

Karen speaks of Ronnie's "otherworldliness." During the interview she looked at him and said, "You still have that effect on me." It's easy to see why. In this interview you'll hear about their never-ending courtship and their constant celebration of love.

Philip: You've been married how long?

Ronnie: Ninety years.

Karen: Twenty-six years.

Ronnie: Oh, well we've known each other thirty-six.

Karen: I know that I met Ronnie... I met him when I was twelve.

Ronnie: I'm jealous of those twelve years before. What happened? I keep asking your parents.

Philip: Let's start with this question: What sort of things can you know about someone after twenty-six years that you wouldn't have known after fifteen years?

Ronnie: Nothing.

Marilyn: Nothing?

Ronnie: You don't know anything. You're always starting over. It's always courtship. It's in another realm. This is the greatest gift in the world. You're in Wonder. You have always this notion that you're just starting — I don't know anything until now. It is wonderful. That's the greatest gift of being alive; it's being in love.

And so, you start again and say, "Wow. Who are you? You're so fascinating." There's so much. There's just wonder. Love allows you to live in a dimension where there's nothing but the privilege of being close. It's God's gift.

From the beginning, there was magic. I just knew it was destiny. This line and only this line. When we met, with love, it was important for me to reduce myself. I was more a teacher than an equal. At the same time I also loved how she admired me and how Karen was so close to me. She would look with kind of a sparkle when I was teaching. She always had her eyes on me but not as any more than as a teacher.

	Even so I believed that I am, and was, accepted on a very ethereal level by Karen. So, I hold the highest pedestal, the highest regard, toward Karen. At the same time I know that my role is to take her out of the practical world, the world that she's so competent in.
	My role is more to be a force for her in a poetic, sublime interaction. And I think that's where we came together. There was always an awareness that we were more to each other than what anyone else could see.
Philip:	**When did you have that awareness that Karen was the one? When did it dawn?**
Ronnie:	When I allowed it. I allowed it. I allowed it.
	We were in a Zionist youth group together. I was a minor celebrity in that group and there was a point where she came of age and she wasn't twelve anymore and I noticed her. I knew, and I know, that she has endless dimension. She has infinity inside her.
	And so, I told her about it. We were walking on a field, in a baseball field, walking and talking. We had spent a lot of time talking and exploring and expressing ourselves. It was wonderful but it wasn't mutual.
	Then at a certain point she was of age and I wasn't anymore in that teacher position. She was going to Israel and I felt a strong loss anticipating her going into the greater world. She had taken a lot of my teachings and lot of the romance of my teachings into her life and she was now, kind of, launching. And I felt that it's time – it became intimate.
	She was seventeen and I'm five years older. You were seventeen?
Karen:	Yeah, you were twenty-two.
Philip:	So this is when the relationship between you changed?

Ronnie: Uh-huh.

Philip: And how did it change? What did you say?

Ronnie: I kissed her.

Marilyn: *(To Karen)* Were you surprised?

Karen: First let me back up a bit and set the stage. The first time I saw him, I was twelve and it was at a Zionist camp. I remember sitting in this open field, a different field than the one where we fell in love.

But there was some Texas, brushy woods and I see this figure moving through the woods. Ronnie walked like a gazelle. He moved with one leg out and then pulled it in very straight, walking solo in the distance through these woods. I was mesmerized. I remember just thinking, "Who is that? Who is that creature?"

Then he came and he was absolutely such an Other Kind of Force, an Otherworldliness in some way. I saw him, I would say, definitely pedestal style, looking up. *(To Ronnie)* You still have that effect on me. You still have that effect on other people, I think. Also he always had this ... there was a child that was with him. He would lead discussions and there was a child with him, a child with Down syndrome, who was maybe six or seven. And he would hold her hand while he was teaching and he was eighteen years old. She would look up at him and then they would walk out and he would bring her everywhere. It was Ronnie's sister. And that was where I made this other assessment. What teenager would not feel in some way burdened or stigmatized to bring his mentally challenged sister with him everywhere he went?

He would always bring her along and she looked at him so longingly and he was so gentle that I really felt that this was not only somebody who had great things to teach but somebody who had great humanity.

Marilyn: **So the first kiss was five years later. Did you see it coming?**

Karen: Absolutely not. I'm extremely loyal and I'm very bounded. My sexuality doesn't flow out of my relationship. It's contained. I don't think I ever give off to anybody messages of openness. I think it's very innate. It's like I don't see outside the structure. And I don't try to play with the structure.

So Ronnie was in a counselor kind of role. It didn't occur to me to see beyond that. I mean, I never thought of Ronnie in that way at all. I thought of him as somebody who had something to teach. And we worked together.

Our group had been out at someone's lake for a weekend program and it started pouring and maybe we were 40 or 50 people at a lake house. It wasn't working because there wasn't space to be indoors. So we came back to Dallas.

It was evening, the program was over and we started to just take this walk, Ronnie and I, just talking about programs, about ideas, about life. Ronnie was full of philosophy.

I think the walk was probably until about four o'clock in the morning. We started this walking back and forth, back and forth. And as we were talking – I don't know all of the subjects that we covered – but there was a kind of an energy that kept moving and there was an intensity through these hours and hours. We just came to this place of magic.

I wouldn't have seen it coming before I started the walk and by the end, there was nothing more obvious.

It was probably around April when this happened and I was graduating high school. The following year I was planning to spend in Israel. I was leaving in September. So we went back and forth quite a bit that summer.

Then Ronnie said the most beautiful thing anybody could ever say to somebody. He said, "Go." This was something he always said until we really committed our lives together. He said, "You're going away for the year and you'll see. If you find something better than what we have, then you're blessed. Otherwise, we'll come back together."

And we always corresponded. Ronnie is a poet, and he sent beautiful love poetry. But we – he set the model of freeing each other. When we were not together, we could try and find the perfect love. So, I had relationships, Ronnie had relationships. We did that a few times where we weren't in the same environment. I was in Israel for a year and came back. And then Ronnie was in Israel for the next two years actually. It took about eight years.

Ronnie: Our parents decided.

Karen: Our parents told us. [Laughter] Our parents brought us together. They said, "We think it's time."

Ronnie: So we had a ceremony for preparing ourselves to be married. We created ceremonies for the parents.

Karen: Yeah, both of our parents were there.

Ronnie: They gave us blessings. Usually when Jews have these ceremonies it's a year before the wedding.

Philip: I've been Jewish all my life and I've never heard of this.

Ronnie: Yeah. The T'naim. It's called, in English, "The Conditions." It's a ceremony. It's a time of spending time with the families and then really vowing and understanding the depth of Promise and the ultimate nature of Promise.

You're held to it very strongly. You have to really do internal and preparatory work. You create the structure of the home that you'll build. This is your involvement with the seriousness of relationship.

We wrote out our conditions ourselves. We got blessings from each of our parents. We took a plate and smashed it on the ground and said "This is complete now." It's very dramatic and beautiful.

Really the greatest thing in life is to promise, especially for Jews – Promised Land, Promised People, the Promises of Life, the vows of Being, the relationship with God. And so we never know how the future will be but you can always remind each other of that promise. "And don't forget – don't forget what you said; be aware, be conscious." And so that ceremony really profoundly sealed the direction.

And the families picked up the shards of the broken plate and placed them together and it was very, very beautiful.

Two different families, two different stories. It's amazing how close we are. Actually we've found out in Europe we have relatives. We are related to each other.

It was finding how, why, God brought us together because it wasn't really obvious.

The age difference obviously isn't right and odd a bit. And Karen as you can see, as everyone knows, is so beautiful but very, very, reserved about and unaware of her beauty. She has through her whole life been quiet, just watching, and listening, not in any way pushing herself forward. And people really allowed her to be in the background a lot. Most people slid over her. But she was always thinking, always aware, always working, churning with her soul and into everything.

So, because I noticed that, I knew that God had brought us together. I knew that it was soul language and soul discussion. I noticed that her soul was speaking all the time.

I think what we're supposed to do with each other is to say, "You're the one, and you're the only one in the world," to make each other exclusive.

So, even though I gave her that gift to go and try, I knew that it was an exclusivity that I'd found in her. But I've always honored it, to keep it true.

But the ceremony defined it for us. And so it was really very, very beautiful. And the holiness of that moment was a blessing from family and a gift back to the family.

Marilyn: **What were you promising each other?**

Ronnie: How I'll always honor and how there are certain things I would never do. There are certain things I would never say. Love conditions. You've given me so much precious. I'll honor where you're frail or where you're in your own secret world. And you've given me, allowed me, that closeness, so that I'll always honor it.

We build up from the bottom. To honor is to know what not to do and what not to say to each other. And what's tender and what's been preserved or kept very, very much only for each other and that is sacred.

It's a sacred safety that we give to each other, I hope, and which I've tried to teach. When I marry other couples, I've tried to teach them to really, really honor that gift that someone has given you, the gift of their vulnerability.

So those conditions, "T'naim," were part of our own secret. It's not necessarily written out and given out to the world.

	And so we keep asking ourselves how we can be urging each other to our own growth, to our own emerging of ourselves? "How can I be the one that you've entrusted to? How can I be the person that you already see? And how can I be the one that allows you to push me towards places that I've kept bounded?" And that's the gift of why this is an eternal love. Because we're starting over every time, constantly seeing each other, just right now, with the promise still being very active.
Philip:	**How could you have known so much about love when you were so young?**
Ronnie:	My parents loved each other so deeply. I saw the greatest of loves. My father walked across Israel just to see my mother. She came from the most broken, broken losses, from concentration camps as a young child.
	She was seventeen when she came to Israel, and he knew her, and saw her, and he told her that she's so beautiful. People had told her she's an animal and she's the lowest of them, and he said, "You're the most beautiful woman."
	And I knew that I couldn't live on any other plane but with that kind of love because it would be truth. So what they had, I prayed for all my life.
	So I articulate in that language continually. I know a family. They're just ordinary run-of-the-mill walkabouts doing the world with its harsh scratches. But when they come into their home, at home they only whisper. It's the only language that they have in their house. They would never call off to another room, one to each other. They just whisper to each other, "Wow, it's you." And when I find, and realize, that people are doing their love in such a majestic way, I try to incorporate that into our story.
	There's only one story. It's your love story.

And I know that there were people that were hurt when I decided to marry Karen and didn't marry them.

And Karen also had many suitors all the time. Many wanted marriage with Karen. There were people that wanted to join into the love that they thought was meant for them. There was hurt. We still have to care about them. We're still attending to and taking care of people who were hurt in the past.

I know that there was a large price for our love to be. It has to be great. It has to be soulful.

I think this love is dangerous. It should be. Just like God, like God, it is dangerous. You can't be willy-nilly with other people's souls.

Karen: The intensity. I was very attracted to the intensity. I think I hungered for the intensity. My father had been a refugee and my mother's family had been immigrants.

I think somewhere, somehow, there was something of trying to cover over intensity. I think my father's experience coming out of being a refugee was to control for sameness and not have too much high drama.

My parents seemed to have a good marriage, but on reflection, I think it worked well for them because they didn't engage so much. Where they actually got very excited about each other is when they would go away and they would travel and explore. I think they fell in love with each other when they would travel with other people. And then my father would become extremely charming and my mother loved that.

My mother was a good conversationalist and he enjoyed seeing that in her. And so then, against the lens of being out and being curious and being exploring, they would fall in love with each other again.

They would go to theater and they would go to opera, and they enjoyed music and culture together. There was a smell in the house when they were sprucing up, getting ready to go out. There was Shalimar perfume in the air.

So I had a sense that my father really was in love with my mother; he thought she was absolutely, absolutely beautiful, and that was important. Then she thought he was so smart, and that was beautiful. And he thought she was really brilliant, too. But my father worked an hour away and he worked six days a week. And he would leave at 7:30 in the morning and would come back at six for dinner, and we would eat dinner. And there wasn't that much engaging.

On the other hand Ronnie and I, we took a two-year honeymoon. After we married, we traveled for two years. It gave us an amazing foundation with each other. I don't think we felt the great urge to go away to spend time together the way my parents had that urge. We also spend much more time together throughout the day.

You know, I'm thinking about that first question you asked. What struck me was there are things that you learn about somebody after twenty-six years but not after fifteen. And it's through the lens of the family project.

After twenty-six years we're launching our children. We had five kids over ten years, so we're still very much in it. But one of these days they're not all going to be living at home, and we're excited about that again.

I mean we absolutely, absolutely loved the family project. But as it's winding down in the form it's been, I'm learning things about Ronnie, and I see his intensity with his children, that I think I didn't see at the fifteen-year mark.

For me, it's seeing that core person, again, all the way through. I think it's just interesting to see Ronnie in relation to adult children. I think he has the relationships with them in this mentoring kind of role that I saw as he mentored younger people when we were much younger. He takes that role with them, and they look to him for that, and that's really beautiful. I didn't see that as much through the middle years with the younger children. I think the middle years were more challenging years for Ronnie.

I remember moving into a sizeable home after having lived in an apartment for five years when we had the last two children. We moved from Sweden to Toronto and into this sizeable home. So finally, I thought, it won't be four kids in one room. Everybody will have their space and privacy. And we moved into this home and we were like a glob. Wherever we would go, everybody would go together. I anticipated everyone was going to spread out but nobody wanted to. Everybody clung to each other. "Okay, let's have this organic organism move into the kitchen now." Or one would say, "I think I'm going here." "Me, too." "Me, too." And then we would go. "Let's do this together."

So we had this kind of, and still do in many ways, this kind of clan thing that we sort of clan together. The kids, they spindle around each other and they sit on each other's laps and they twist around each other. They're like very, very connected. I think, as they're older and they head off on their own adventures, you know, there is a...

Ronnie: And they love adventure.

Karen: They love adventure, yeah.

Ronnie: And their own LOVE adventures that they're coming to. It is wonderful to see their quests, their fears. The language of the home is always a discourse of love. "What do you need to be a person that can give love? Can I be a person that loves greatly? How to be honoring and not to cheat in love?"

It's a model. I think it's the only thing to really talk about from a religious point of view, too. I want to always *try* to be ready for anyone within our family who asks; the request to be attended to, to be noticed.

Philip: Can that be overdone? We were talking with another couple and he complained that she was always reading his mind and he felt invaded.

Karen: I think there's something about trying not to call someone to where they're not ready to go and being in touch with that place. Yes, we're gently urging each other but we try to not have an agenda.

Ronnie: I think people live in a comfort zone of closeness and distance. Sometimes it's accordion-like and you just need to chase. Sometimes when you are being pursued, you turn back, and sometimes you keep going a little more. And it goes inward and outward.

Everyone does have something that they're preserving yet to the future. If someone peers too closely, the other person might not be ready. So, that's a very important negotiation. Some people need to do the inviting.

Karen: It should be safe. It's important not to threaten; maybe to goad, maybe to urge, maybe to encourage; but not to threaten.

Ronnie: If we talk intimacy, which is failing all around the world, I don't want it to be our failure with each other.

Karen: Talking about vulnerability, I look at it like this: Ronnie calls this "Home." (*She gestures to the space between her heart and Ronnie's*). This is "Home." We traveled for two years and we were always at "Home" wherever we went because we were together.

Ronnie: I think everyone wants so deeply to be known. To be known just as is; I think that's what's built into Shabbat, into the system of Shabbat. This is a time of eternal paradise. And it's just strolling together because "that's the only person I want to be with."

I can't wait for that. Every Shabbat we bless each other. Every Shabbat we tell each other our secrets about them, and their secrets.

To give the blessing to someone, it's hard. It's hard to say, "I know this, I saw what was going on this week. I know you. I'm involved and I want more of it. I want it to come forward, don't hide."

So with younger kids, as Karen was saying, I think we're always interpreting the world for them. "What is reality? What is the story? What is it that I'm experiencing?"

And we put a valance on it: "This is important; this is what our family sees as important." That's how we educate: to go through all these sensations that can happen with reality. We ask them to ask themselves, "How do we interpret a successful negotiation with society?"

But then at a certain point, children want a lot more and they want another reality and the best of reality. And that's when we have this new conversation with them. It's not about just successfully negotiating the adult world or their peer world, but negotiating, really, God's World.

Marilyn: God's World?

Ronnie:	Yes. It's a private story of whatever you resist or whatever you interact with, with your own life force, in your own soul language. It's a private story of how thankful you are to your life, how gratefully you live in the World of Splendor.
	Everyone has their own different nuances to that. And so that shouldn't be imposed from the outside. What's mine isn't yours, I have to honor that.
	But I do know that Judaism does give the world the understanding that God expects something from you, that there is a push for high, high growth for that ethereal world. It should be a Garden, of course. It should be something so magnificent. And so there is a sense of reward in Judaism.
	I love the structure of being able to tell my story with each person, helping each of my children, my wife and I, in our interpretation, our legend with God.
	And that's what we've always implanted in our children, that God language. And now they want to try it out. I think I want to teach my children a kind of eternal trust and not just a temporal reflection on time.
Marilyn:	**So if a spiritual calling is this "pushing you to a higher growth," as you put it, can you give us an example? How has your relationship challenged and pushed each of you?**
Ronnie:	We're in the time now where we are taking care of parents and I watch Karen with just, really, amazement.
	She is so, so delicate with my family and her family and our family and with everyone where their stories are. When I see Karen touching anywhere or anyone, I see again, I see again, that she, her touch, is urged on by God, and it works. It works so beautifully.

Karen:	I think, I mean I think we raise each other. We have really different qualities. We work each other as we go through life.
	Ronnie is completely spontaneous. Yes? Very spontaneous. I'm less spontaneous so I fell in love with Ronnie's spontaneity. And I'm challenged by Ronnie's spontaneity. I think I try to live up to it. But Ronnie is still much more spontaneous.
	And Ronnie is 'Yes'; he's both spontaneous and he's 'Yes'. So if you put those together and you put that together with being in the Rabbinate and then there's everybody's 'Yes' and everybody is spontaneous and everybody is always welcome... but I think I've asked for just a little bit more control, a little bit. Yes, we love an open home, so we always have an open door, people flowing in and out, day, night, whoever, whenever. I love that. I love the life which that brings.
Ronnie:	I've never seen the day that Karen was in the bluster of the void. I chose her. I know her only in joy. I only know her joy. I've never seen her not dance. I've never seen her ... I've never seen you in a way of despair.
	I've never seen the world of loss that you've absorbed into your skin. You know how to really glide into life so beautifully, always.
Philip:	We hear so much about how you are always saying "yes" to each other. What about your "no"?
Karen:	Ronnie doesn't say 'No'. I get a call from someone, it is 2 o'clock in the morning, and I say, "I need to go to my friend's. You just sleep." And he says, "Okay, I'll take you." He 'Yes's' everything. There's no 'No.'
Marilyn:	**Could you tell us about the challenge of dealing with your differences? Do you ever get tangled up in stuff, you know, a "Love Tangle"?**

Ronnie:	The Love Tangle is spaghetti, the will to tangle together and to be involved. It's not the tangle of a narrower heart, no. It's a tangle of, "I can't wait to entwine with you".
Karen:	I don't know, I think we're still growing up, somewhere. *[Turning to Ronnie]* Ronnie, do you have loss?
Ronnie:	I was raised in a holocaust family. I was raised by parents who were orphans. So I was raised by a world that pushed away the void and then lived a kind of fantasy inside their own love. I completely believe in your love, I completely believe in your wondrous, gorgeous sense of dancing in life. And I just want to be part of it. I try to catch up; I try to catch up to that. I learn all the time. You're a fantastic teacher. What a privilege I got to be that close to you. There is a naïveté to love. It's a wonderful belief, knowing what to overlook, and to be in the privilege of a kiss, of a breath.
Karen:	Well, maybe that's the thing about the polarity between us. When I lean toward the "Spontaneous! Yes!", then I know I lean toward him. Whatever those qualities are, it's ethereal. My mother used to say, "You know, Ronnie is an El Greco. Everything is elongated and long." And she'd say, "He is hyperbolic. Everything with him is 'Magnificent!'" When I said I was inspired by the intensity, I was inspired by the extremes also. And, you know, with him everything is 'very' and it's 'very' and it's 'very,' you know?
Ronnie:	Very ultimate.

Karen: *"Meh-od"*, you know the Hebrew word? He is a lot of *"Meh-od"* (Hebrew for "very"), A lot of just fullness. So, it's to fall in love, over and over again with what I fell in love with originally. I think we don't change really, I mean, what we are is what our essence is. It's the 360 degrees of what I might encounter that made me look at it through one lens or another lens. But there is a space lens that sees it all. I fell in love with Ronnie through that lens, so it's to return to that place.

Ronnie: I see no polarity. I see exactly where that meets and it's exactly perfect. It's perfect.

Karen: I think with those different qualities we're constantly learning from each other because we bond. And particularly at midlife you bump into your limitations. Maybe there's a grounding, maybe that's my function, as more of an anchor piece or something. But I keep always being reminded of The Possible with Ronnie.

Marilyn: I'm going to sing you my ditty that's about what we were talking about.

Karen: Yes.

Marilyn: (Singing)
*The one thing I love the most
about the one that I love
is the way he embraces parts of me
I know not of.*

I was reminded of it when you two were talking about your Shabbas rituals of discovering each other.

Karen : Shabbas is so beautiful...

Ronnie: Seductive.

Karen: Because it's about that time where everything else falls away and it's just inner time.

Ronnie: It's such a gift.

Marilyn: I guess some people just do the falling away part on Sabbath. They miss that part where you bring in everything else. They miss where you always re-discover each other.

Karen: It's so radical. Really.

Ronnie: We have the same dreams. Either we talk in our sleep…

Marilyn: When you have five kids, I guess that's when you have to meet. I'll meet you in a dream tonight.

Ronnie: We can wake up and finish each other's dreams. We're very much in a very long and beautiful dialogue about each other. And actually, we wrote that in our wedding invitations. "I am yours and my dreams are yours." And so that night world is as important to me, to us, as the day-to-day practical. That's what I meant by the courtship.

Marilyn: And the courtship is… how you win her over? What is courtship for you?

Karen: I'm so easy.

Ronnie: That we're continually in the courtship, trying again, and looking and starting over. I love it. I love that privilege, because it's so fascinating to commit to that. It's so beautiful. It's not ever just satisfied. Because I mean I'm blessed all the time because of the future. I'm blessed always.

Prayer prepares you. Every day's prayer prepares you for that privilege. "Oh, this is the reason for the day. This is the wondrous gift, a way I could be a part of you." So it's kind of being on the lookout for the awareness of the magic and the world opens up to us. And we are so blessed and so, so truly given it all.

In August 2011, Rabbi Cahana suffered a stroke. He could only blink his eyes. Five days after this event he blinked out his first sermon to his congregation. With the support of his wife and family and congregants he has been slowly, steadily, and even miraculously, recovering.

In 2013 He was quoted in Time magazine in a photo story by his daughter, Kitra Cahana. **http://kitracahana.com/**

Here is a quote from Ronnie published in that article.

"You have to believe you're paralyzed to play the part of a quadriplegic; I don't in my mind and in my dreams every night I Chagall-man float over the city, twirl and swirl. With my toes kissing the floor. I know nothing about this statement of man without motion. Everything has motion. The heart pumps, the bloods race course, the lungs culminate, the body heaves, the mouth moves, the eyes turn inside-out. We never stagnate. Life triumphs up and down." —Rabbi Cahana Montreal, Quebec, 2013.

Rabbi Ronnie is the Rabbi at Congregation Beth-El in Montreal, QC. ***hhtp://www.beth-elmtl.org/***

His sermons and poetry and other writings are on his website, as well as the audio of this interview.
http://rabbicahana.com/

Rabbi Ronnie and Karen
The Blue Thread in Their Love Story

Come my Beloved. It is the Sabbath. Let us welcome her.
Don't be unhappy, don't be downcast.
Come in peace. Be Glad. Be joyful.
It's the Sabbath. Enter, dear Bride, enter.
-- Lecha Dodi (Sung every Sabbath)

In every couple's Genesis story, their spontaneously remembered and cherished story of their first encounter, we can get a glimpse of how they hold the promise of their relationship.

In Karen's Genesis story she remembers the moment she first saw Ronnie and her imagination was captured. She was twelve years old.

Karen: This figure moving through the woods ... like a gazelle ... Who is that? Who is that creature?" ... absolutely such an Other Kind of Force, an other-worldliness.

For her there was a promise of moving beyond the quotidian into an "other world," beyond the mundane and into the poetic.

For Ronnie, that Genesis moment when the ordinary relationship crystallized into something magical happened later when Karen was 17. He invited her to walk with him.

Ronnie: I knew that God had brought us together. I knew that it was soul language and soul discussion ... So I told her about it. We were walking on a field, in a baseball field, walking and talking. ... I kissed her.

So that image of the two of them walking, late at night, under a starry sky, talking soul language, in a timeless moment, this is how Ronnie still sees their possibilities.

Again and again, in so many ways, they share with us glimpses into a poetic and sublime time where Love would be recognized as a holy and special state. It would be a time outside, but also inside, ordinary time.

In those moments, everything would be new, always new, always filled with wonder, and a gift from God. Vulnerability would be honored and cherished. Love could flourish in safety.

That's what the ceremony of the *T'naim* was about, stating the conditions under which Love could continue to flower. The Conditions were, in effect, promises they were making to each other about how they would be with each other always.

> Ronnie: *I'll honor where you're frail or where you're in your own secret world. ... And what's tender and what's been preserved or kept very, very much only for each other. ... It's a sacred safety that we give to each other, to really honor ... the gift of their vulnerability.*

But it's not enough to just promise. Every week, every Sabbath, they set aside a time only for them, sacred, "away from the bluster of the void." Within that special time, they raise each other up. They cherish each other, they love each other, they reveal to each other their tender secrets. In that safe haven they remember again and again "Why God brought us together," and where they want to go, and where they can go.

> Ronnie: *How can we be urging each other to our own growth, to our own emerging of ourselves? "How can I be the one that you've entrusted to? And how can I be the one that allows you to push me towards places that I've kept bounded?"*

They are also quite aware of the fine line between encouraging the best in a partner and merely nagging. They emphasize how careful one must be.

> Karen: *It's important not to threaten; maybe to goad, maybe to urge, maybe to encourage; but not to threaten.*

> Ronnie: *Because we're starting over every time, constantly seeing each other, Just right, just now... with the promise still being very active.*

This commitment and practice of deepening their intimacy is the blue thread.

When we look at this blue thread, we are reminded of how the tender parts of love must be protected and nurtured and that, when this is done, love becomes rapture.

Ronnie: *So it's kind of being on the lookout for the awareness of the magic and the world opens up to us. And we are so blessed and so, so truly given it all.*

Chapter Two

This Love,
Like the Moon in All Its Phases

Rabbi Leibish and Deena Hundert

> *There needs to be a sense of exile within the relationship, a sense of separateness within it because you still are separate people. You can delude yourself with over-familiarization and lose that sense of individual exile within the marriage. And then you lose this sense of reunion and excitement. – Rabbi Leibish*

> *I remember under the Chuppah when the glass was broken and we were officially married we held on to each other's hand and that was the first time we were ever touching. We were holding hands. I just remember feeling like a million dollars. I was like, "This is all I need." I'm just gonna hold hands forever and I'm never letting go. – Deena*

Apart. Together. Apart. Together. This rhythm runs through their relationship. At this point they can't imagine one state without the other. As you read their stories, even if you are miles away from orthodox practice, you'll be able to appreciate why they treasure this cycle and what they gain from it.

Deena and Leibish observe *Niddah*, which means that each lunar month there are 14 days in which they are strictly separate. It's a very orthodox practice. No touching, not even to pass the salt.

Deena and Leibish share with us the significance of this practice for them, how it enriches so much more than just their sex life.

As you hear their stories, you will see the challenges as well as the gifts of this practice.

Marilyn: **When did you actually think, "Wow, this person could be a significant person in my life?"**

Deena: On one of our dates, I think it was our second one, I remember we were walking in the streets and we ran into some friends of his. That day was someone's *Yarzheit* (anniversary of a death). And right away he gave over a little Torah, a little talk about that person.

Later we sat down somewhere and I left for a minute and when I came back, he was saying some Psalms.

Just those two things were very impressionable on me. Like, "This is someone that I want. I want someone to be like that."

You know, you arrive with friends and instead of just having small talk, he is like, "Let's make this moment holy and talk about something significant. And in spare moments let's do something productive, or holy or whatever." That was just a sign to me, "Okay. This is for me."

And then it just became more and more apparent to the point where I was just waiting for him to realize that too. *(Laughter)*

Leibish: For me, there were two stories. One story is on our very first date. We went to this house in Jerusalem to visit my high school teacher, Reb Shalom, a very close person to me. My rational mind was not at all thinking of things like, "Is this the one or not?" I was just getting to know her. I was introducing her, "This is Deena," and suddenly it felt like this was a momentous moment.

Deena: You wanted to say this is my wife or something?

Leibish: Yeah, I don't know if I wanted to exactly say that. Maybe. Suddenly, it felt so significant. But I just couldn't handle that right away.

So I just closed it up and closed it up very tightly.

Then there's that other story a week or two later, when we went to visit my great aunt and my shirt was sticking out. And Deena was saying, "Are you a shirt-sticking-out person or a shirt-tucked-in person?" And I remember thinking, like, "Wow. If that was anybody else asking this question that would be the end of the relationship." I would not take that from anybody. If I was going to make a list of the type of things I was looking for in a person, I would never put "Somebody who cares and is concerned about my physical appearance" on that list. In fact it would have been a turn-off, like, "What do you care? It's my shirt. Either it's in or it's out. Leave it alone." But somehow because it was from her I was, like, "Okay, however you want it to be."

And that was very big. That was for my rational mind and easier to digest than the totality of introducing her to Reb Shalom.

Marilyn: What a sign of love it is when you could be willing to say, "Okay, that's not me, but that's fine. I'm willing to be that. I'm you're man."

Leibish: Well, to just even care about it at all. To this day the fact that I tuck my shirts in is only because of her. It's still not really a part of me.

Deena: I guess it is something that you care about, especially if you're representing Torah. Especially as a Rabbi you should look respectful. You shouldn't look like you just rolled out of bed.

Marilyn: You wanted the tucking-in type person, right?

Deena: Not always. But I definitely prefer the shirt tucked out than a shirt with one side in and one side out.

Philip: Well, how long have you been together now?

Deena: Six years.

Leibish: Yeah, six.

Deena: We had our sixth anniversary in June.

Philip: What do you know about each other after six years that you didn't know earlier?

Deena: We've definitely gone through some hard spots.

Leibish: And gone through some stuff.

Deena: And we're in a much different place than we were four years ago.

Leibish: I realized that being in a relationship brings out a lot of stuff that isn't actually about the relationship. It's like acting out older pain. That was something that we went through. Almost tore us apart.

Deena: Being in a relationship actually creates a safe space for negative stuff to come out. If you're single it feels like, "Well I'll be safer if I go back to being single." Probably it's really not true. It's just that being single I can keep it under the carpet better.

Leibish: I was really doubting the relationship, deeply. I was freaking out. I thought that it was so sad that I'd have to hurt such a great person and this is so terrible but I just can't do this anymore.

We went to a Rabbi in Jerusalem, and he talked to me and he asked me about Deena and all I had to say was positive. So he said, "You've got to go to therapy. Because, if there's nothing actually wrong and you just feel like you need to get out of this, then there's got to be something else that needs to be worked on."

And it was very frightening for Deena and for me because we didn't know what it was and what was going on. Basically the real thing came from my uncle who was a therapist.

He gave us this concept of the safe space which is a hugely redeeming idea that the negativity actually speaks well of the relationship. The fact that I can talk, that all this pain is coming out is because I feel safer now for it to come out.

That turned everything around and helped Deena understand. It also helped me understand. And whenever couples are getting married I often share with them this idea of the safe space.

	Because there's one thing I learned through this, that what seems to be the logical choice of separating is actually completely wrong. That was an amazing realization.
Deena:	I don't know if you know that we went through losing a child together. And that was something that has bound us together, to go through that experience together. We would sit in the hospital and we would hear these things daily, people saying "This is wrong and yet this is happening." Some days would be better days than others.
Leibish:	And sometimes it was crazy.
Deena:	But the fact that we were able to hold on to each other... We would sit in the waiting room or even sit in the hospital and sit next to her, next to our daughter in her little... What's it called?
Leibish:	Incubator.
Deena:	Incubator for a while. And we would just sit there. And the fact that we could have each other, hold on to each other through this...
	Unfortunately, we witnessed other couples getting torn apart in situations like this. And today it's really sad for me because the wife in one of these couples, who I am still friendly with, she still has her son because he survived, but now she doesn't have anyone to raise him with. It's really painful and hard. Her son is like a constant reminder of her husband.
	Whereas, us, we don't have a daughter, but we have each other. And, *Baruch Ha Shem* (Blessed is God), we have two beautiful children now. So I feel really grateful that we were able to just talk to *Ha Shem* and thank *Ha Shem* for helping us through that process. In fact, we were strengthened through it.
Philip:	Was that before or after the discovery of the safe space?
Deena:	Oh, after. Yeah.

Leibish: We probably wouldn't have been able to handle it had we not first done that work. Anytime that I would get triggered and start freaking out that it was actually...

Deena: It wasn't about me.

Leibish: It wasn't about you at that moment. But the fact that I was able to experience those emotions and wasn't piling them up was actually a testament to the fact that the relationship was good.

Philip: Could you describe how you handled it in this new way?

Leibish: It just means I have a voice in my head that is saying, "Okay, this is an overreaction and I know it's an overreaction."

Deena: I think what we try and do now is not talk when we're getting into one of those spaces. Take some space. Come again and talk again once we've calmed down and once we're not in the emotional winds.

One of us would just walk out of the room or leave the house.

Leibish: But we'll talk about it, sometimes at the moment, sometimes afterwards.

Deena: Usually afterwards.

For me, if something is upsetting me, I'll say to him, "I don't want to be talking to you this way and I don't want to be feeling this way.

But I just can't handle anymore. I know that I don't want to be a wife like this. I don't want to be someone that's nagging or who is making you feel bad or wrong about yourself. But, I don't know how."

I'm constantly asking you to help me know how to say things that won't trigger you in a negative way. I'm conscious that sometimes there's a way that I speak that actually pushes you away, and that's not helping anything.

	So I have to learn how to choose my words and choose my tone. A lot of times it's my tone, I think.

So I have to learn how to choose my words and choose my tone. A lot of times it's my tone, I think.

I know that he really loves me and appreciates me for what I bring to the relationship. I think I used to just feel everything was about me. I used to think all these horrible things about myself. I still definitely have moments of having my own self-esteem issues, but now at least I know that he is really happy with his choice of me as his partner. If anything, he thanks me all the time for helping him to achieve milestones and get to places.

Right now we just had a graduation on Monday for his Master's degree. This was hard work for him but it was also hard work for me.

Leibish: It was hard work for you.

Deena: Not in the sense of writing papers or going to class or doing research but in pushing him to meet deadlines and to actually get the stuff done, and to make sure he pays the balance. I do everything I need to in order to make it happen.

Leibish: And tuck my shirt in.

Marilyn: That's totally what I was thinking. In certain ways you're keeping him on track which is great. And in other ways it could be construed as nagging.

Deena: Right, sometimes it's negative. Exactly.

Marilyn: It's a double-edged sword.

Philip: Do you have a story for us about how your Judaism affects your relationship and vice versa?

Leibish: When we were first dating we were talking about the parts of Judaism that speak to us the most deeply. What I found the deepest in Judaism is an acknowledgment of Lack. There was a crying out about the destruction of the temple. For me, at the base of my being, I want to be playing music in Jerusalem.

I'm a *Levi* (from the line of Priests) and I want to be in the band and doing my thing. The world is so far from that.

For Deena, what draws her most to Judaism is thankfulness and gratitude. That's a complete opposite to Lack.

I remember Deena saying one time on the phone, that in our depths we are just different. At that moment it sounded like we were not supposed to go together, but then I said, "No. I think that we really both need each other." That was something.

Deena: What triggered me just now was remembering that, first, before we were married, we didn't have a physical relationship at all.

People would always ask, "How do you get to know about a guy and his intimacy if you're not going to be together first?" One of my mentors would say, "Watch the way he handles creatures, other creatures, animals, the spider. Watch the way he interacts with people. Watch. Is he gentle?" You just look. Watch him in all the different other relationships and encounters and you get to see a lot about a person through that.

I remember, when under the *Chuppah* (the marriage canopy), when the glass was broken and we were officially married, we held on to each other's hand and that was the first time we were ever touching. We were holding hands.

I just remember feeling like a million dollars. I was like, "This is all I need." I'm just gonna hold hands forever and I'm never letting go. And it was an amazing moment and I remember that feeling so vividly because I did wait for that point. We waited.

Marilyn: So once you got married, you kept the Orthodox ritual of Niddah?

Philip: What's Niddah?

Deena: Basically, when a woman is menstruating, she is not physical at all with her husband. There are even some gates around that. There is no touching, so you put a gate around it and don't even pass each other objects. Because doing that makes you want to touch.

It basically happens for around two weeks. One week when you just can't be together. Then there's a week after that of preparation to be together, the clean days where you are now waiting. You are completely done with your period but you are now just in this counting process. You count seven days until you can go to the *Mikvah* (ritual bath) and then you can be together again. So it ends up being about two weeks of the month where you're not really physical at all.

So then, after coming home from the *Mikvah*, it's really like another wedding night. From not being together at all for so long, now you get to be together again. It's this amazing experience. It brings you back. I even have a lotion that I don't wear all the time but I put on when I come back from the Mikvah. And I'll put on the outfit that I wore on our wedding night. It brings us right back.

When I just came back from the *Mikvah* after having the baby it was like we were just starting again but so much deeper because now we know each other. We'd gone through so much in our relationship and solved issues. It was like the wedding night times a hundred.

So I feel that Leibish being a Rabbi and our being connected to Jewish law makes for a more intimate and more exciting and more passionate relationship. And it's because of this going away a distance, and coming back, and distance, and coming back ... it's constantly exciting.

Keeping these laws of family purity, this I really believe is the foundation of everything else that goes on in the relationship and marriage.

	For example I just had a baby, right? So after you have a baby you bleed for a while, okay?
	So that means that we're not together, we're not intimate at all. And forget intimate, we're not physical at all during that period.
Philip:	Which means you don't even touch?
Deena:	Right, Not during that period of time while I'm bleeding. So we just recently had a reunion and it had been a few months. I would say that that was very amazing, just like the safe space that we were talking about before. It felt so right and so safe to be together again and be united again and to be one.
	Maybe sometimes I get frustrated about things or get upset, but at the end of the day we do pine for each other. When we are together we feel very at home in an intimate way. If we were together all the time, if we didn't have the separation, then I don't know... When I'm having a down time or if something is upsetting me, when I shut him out... I don't know. How do I put it into words? Leibish, you're good at expressing things.
Leibish:	Well, there needs to be a sense of exile within the relationship, a sense of separateness within it because you really still are separate people. You can delude yourself with over-familiarization and lose that sense of individual exile within the marriage. And then you lose this sense of reunion and excitement.
	I think she's saying that it feels like a very foundational thing, this practice. Because it's outside of ourselves, something divine, something special that constantly brings us closer or separates us. And you always know when the next separation time is coming up. You're within something.
Marilyn:	A cycle.

Leibish:	It gives context to things. It gives staying power. There's something beyond us which our relationship is within. That's really important because without that you can just pretend, "I could do that all the time." "Well, of course we're married, we're happy, tra-la-la."
	It's been two weeks since we even held hands and we've gotten into a fight, but tomorrow night she's going to the *Mikvah*. So we have an added motivator to make up, that sense of a special time coming up.
	When there's a rhythm it helps you to say, "Hey, wait a second …"
Deena:	And it just reminds me of what the real truth is. Really we have a beautiful, amazing, loving connection and the bad stuff is just a detail, something that we have to work on. That's not the core of our relationship.
Leibish:	Yeah. It helps you re-experience and transcend.
Deena:	A lot of the time when we're reunited, when we re-experience us, it's like, "Right, I was upset with you about whatever, that you didn't get that phone call, that you spoke the wrong way, or…
Philip:	So in these reunion moments, do you just set the problems aside and say, "We'll deal with them later because it's been two weeks and…"
Deena:	No, no, no, no. Not at all.
Leibish:	You really have to reconcile stuff.
Deena:	It forces you to talk it out.
Marilyn:	It's another kind of *Mikvah* almost?
Leibish:	Yeah, an emotional *Mikvah*.
Marilyn:	And then you come together?
Leibish:	Absolutely. Like Deena said, "We're getting married again." So if we have a fight during the engagement we're not gonna just go and say, "Well, okay we'll solve it after the wedding is over."

You want to go into that night happy. It becomes very, very important. Every time, almost every time, there has been stuff that we were forced to resolve before coming back together again.

And the same is true for *Shabbas*. For *Shabbas*, unfortunately we don't have as great a track record. With the nights where she goes to the *Mikvah*, we really do have an amazing track record of fixing things before she goes, right?

But in terms of *Shabbas*, that needs more work. Ideally you fix all your relationships before *Shabbas* comes in, because you need to be able to sit with your family and have *Shabbas* together.

Part of the thing, though, of being a Rabbi, in particular a college Rabbi, is that many, many of our Shabbas meals are with fifty to a hundred students.

Deena: And they go late.

Leibish: And so our personal time on *Shabbas* is very small. I don't really think you can raise a family properly this way. Once our kids start getting older I don't want them to grow up in such a public arena. I want them to have *Shabbas* in the classic sense of family peacefulness. So that's gonna be something that we'll have to navigate. What we do have instead of *Shabbas* is a date-night once a week. One thing about being a college Rabbi is that there is an activity almost every night of the week.

Having a night just to ourselves is extremely relaxing but we don't get it often. We don't have normal lives to live where you close the door and think, "I left work." We can't leave work. We're just here.

Students know that they can always just call us. Even at night when there's nothing planned students come over. So we really take advantage of date-night and *Mikvah* night.

	And little by little, more and more, we will take back our family *Shabbas*.
Philip:	So what does a date-night consist of?
Leibish:	I like to go out to dinner. Deena is more frugal. I have very little sense of the value of money. And if I have it, I'll just give it all away or I'll spend it. I'm not particularly proud of the way I deal with money. But anyways, we'll go out for dinner or we'll go for a walk on the mountain across the street or sometimes we'll just stay home.
Deena:	Play a board game.
Leibish:	Chill out, play a board game.
Deena:	And then usually go to bed early and together.
	Yeah.
Marilyn:	**A Rabbi chooses to be a Rabbi. Knowing what you now know, Deena, would you choose to be a Rebbetzin?**
Deena:	I love being this person who can be there for other people who are looking for direction. Before we got married I was a *madricha,* a counselor. I myself didn't grow up observing Jewish Law. Neither of us did. I came to it through a slow process on my own. I feel very grateful to be able to share my own personal experiences with others. So this role, being like a mother of the house, I like that. When we were dating I very well knew that this is what I was getting into and I was excited about it.
	Now as far as *Shabbas* is concerned and not having as much privacy as we would like, I don't go into every *Shabbas* with *Simchah* (rejoicing).
	That is actually a problem because on *Shabbas* it's a *mitzvah* (commandment) to be happy. I have to work on that. And there are some *Shabbases* that I actually resent the fact that we don't get to come home earlier and do our thing and have more time together.

	Also there was a period of time where I couldn't go to Shul because I had the baby at home. Finally we came up with this amazing idea to hire someone to come to watch the baby.
Marilyn:	So you were stuck at home?
Deena:	Right. And he would go and be there and be with everyone and I would just be having my own meal. That really wasn't so great. Now still, I think it was just this last Shabbas that I went with you and then, when we came home, I was so tired I fell asleep. I was so upset with myself.
Leibish:	I wasn't upset. I would have fallen asleep on the table. I forgave her.
Marilyn:	**So being a Rebbetzin has its challenges and rewards. Could you say more about how this relationship brings you to a place you would not have gone on your own?**
Deena:	More connecting and talking to God. If I'm really having a hard day, I just go across the street and walk into the forest and just pour my heart out to *HaShem* (God). I feel so much better. It's like a workout.
	Leibish reminds me to do that. I don't know if I would otherwise. I used to do it in the past but life was just so much calmer when I was single. It's great to have a life filled with activity and the children but definitely I have moments …
Leibish:	Like to carve out the time, yeah.
Deena:	What I do notice is that even stopping to have this conversation today helps me re-focus because some days I am sure that some of my character traits bother him and some of his bother me and sometimes those get highlighted and I get frustrated. Even though at the core I know that this is my soul-mate and I love him to pieces and I am so grateful. I really thank God for sending him to me every single day.
	But I still have these moments where I think, "Why can't you just…" you know. Little things.

But sitting and talking about this reminds me of the point of everything and how I really do feel and how I really am so grateful.

I pray for my friends who are so looking for their soul-mates that they should be able to find them and have the amazing, exciting, passionate, deep relationship that I have.

Leibish: I also feel re-focused. In talking about the "shirt tucked in story," I'm realizing how that actually is not an isolated story but actually represents a direction of work that is important for me to continue to be engaged in, not just for the pure sense of changing myself, but also for the positive end of being more financially responsible and generous. But I am a space cadet. I don't want to say that unqualifiedly. I'm not always, but I tend toward being a bit out of this world. A little bit.

Deena: So that's what attracted me to him. I love that he is so spiritual and so deep and so connected to God but at the same time, I want to say, "Okay! Now it's time to be here."

Marilyn: Just tuck your shirt in! Beautiful.

At the time of the interview, 2010, Reb Leibish had been the Rabbi of the Ghetto Shul connected to McGill University in Montreal, QC. In the interview he'd said, "Our personal time on Shabbas is very small. I don't really think you can raise a family properly this way." Deena also expressed some misgivings. In 2012, Leibish announced that he was quitting the position in order to spend more time with his family. The interview about this decision is at
http://www.cjnews.com/montreal/student-run-ghetto-shul-close

Reb Leibish and Deena
The Blue Thread in Their Love Story

*To everything there is a season,
And a time to every purpose under the heaven:
A time to weep, and a time to laugh; a time to mourn,
And a time to dance.
– Ecclesiastes 3*

We were sitting around a table in a local coffee shop listening to Reb Leibish give seminar about Tisha B'Av, a Jewish holiday commemorating tragic events and marked by mourning and grief. "What about the power of the present moment?" someone asked. This person had just read a book about that and he asked Leibish, "Why can't we just live in the present?"

Leibish said, "We can't. We're Jews. You can't feel exaltation if you are not equally willing to feel grief." This was also how he and Deena constructed their marriage and we saw this in our conversation with them. They were not one of those couples who only wanted a quiet, pleasant haven. They wanted something more deeply felt.

We see this in Deena's Genesis story. She and Leibish, just getting to know each other, ran into friends who were observing the anniversary of someone's death. Leibish did not make small talk. As she put it, "He was like, let's make this moment holy." That struck a chord in her heart and told her he was her man.

Leibish is a man who feels deeply and who also finds this to be a bit challenging. We see this in his Genesis story. When he was introducing Deena to his teacher he said, "Suddenly it felt like this was a momentous moment." He couldn't say *what* was happening, only that *something* was happening, some kind of holy mystery. And then he said, "I just couldn't handle that right away. So I just closed it up and closed it up very tightly."

They both talked about learning to open up to each other but they also talked about the dangers of it, and how it almost split them apart. If they were going to fulfill their love for each other, they were going to have to figure out how to welcome deep feelings and also manage them.

There was something about the external structures they found in Orthodox Judaism that helped them enormously. Both came to it before they met; neither had grown up in an Orthodox context. But it gave them a structure for their love. In Orthodox Judaism there are weekly, monthly and yearly cycles of rituals and in these rituals all the differing colors of the human heart have their place of honor. This made it possible for them to give themselves over to their true emotions and still feel safe.

The *Mikvah,* which they spoke about, was only one example:

Leibish: *This practice, it's outside of ourselves, something divine, something special that constantly brings us closer or separates us. And you always know when the next separation time is coming up. You're within something.*

Rituals like the *Niddah* helped Leibish and Deena open up to powerful cycles like longing and coming together, and like grief and joy that otherwise they might have found overwhelming. After the *Mikvah,* they have what Reb Leibish calls an "emotional *Mikvah*," a conversation which is an emotional cleansing for their relationship. It adds a psychological and emotional dimension that's every bit as important to them as the actual physical ritual.

They also take the basic idea of meaningful separation, the principle behind the Mikvah, and liberate it for their own use, whenever, not just at pre-ordained times. Whenever they are in a bad mood they give each other permission to separate. Since they know that they will talk about it later, separation then becomes a phase in a cycle.

Deena: *I think what we try and do now is not talk when we're getting into one of those spaces. Take some space. Come again and talk again once we've calmed down and once we're not in the emotional winds.*

Leibish: *There needs to be a sense of exile within the relationship, a sense of separateness within it because you really still are separate people. You can delude yourself with over-familiarization and lose that sense of individual exile within the marriage. And then you lose this sense of reunion and excitement.*

In a love relationship feelings change but in a deeper sense they do not; a love relationship has its cycles. This, for us, is the blue thread, that in a relationship there are cycles and we must honor them. An important way we honor the reality of cycles is through rituals. Creating rituals, observing them and fine-tuning them is one of the ways we shape, honor and refine love.

And this takes us to the fine line. Every relationship has its rituals. However, they can be rote and empty or they can be alive and moving. They can constrict life or they can open it up. Leibish and Deena use the prescribed rhythms of Orthodox Judaism to frame and enhance their own natural rhythms. Their rituals do not imprison them. As they go through their cycles of longing and reunion, grief and joy, each phase seems fresh, safe, and more beautiful than the last time.

Deena: So then, after coming home from the Mikvah, it's really like another wedding night... I'll put on the outfit that I wore on our wedding night. It brings us right back. We'd gone through so much in our relationship and solved issues. When I just came back from the Mikvah after having the baby it was like we were just starting again but so much deeper because now we know each other. It was like the wedding night times a hundred.

Chapter Three

Without Touching, Without Gazing, No Intimate Exchange of Words For Seven Years, and Yet...

Rabbi Yisroel and Sara Bernath

For a second, I was walking down the street and I just glanced and we kind of passed an eye. There were thousands of girls, thousands of people. We exchanged glances. That was it. That was it. And this whole time... We're talking about how many years? Seven years. I really had no idea. – Rabbi Yisroel

But even if you don't speak to somebody, you still get a feeling. I mean, if you know a person for that amount of time, you see them that often, if they're in your house every single week even if you don't speak to them, you still-- you still know who they are. – Sara

In the Genesis story, Jacob, whose name was later changed to "Yisroel," sees his beloved for the first time at a well. He falls in love with her instantly but it will be seven years before he can consummate that love. Imagine all those years he spends around her, working for her father, always more or less in her presence. What went on between them during those seven years? The Genesis story doesn't say.

Rabbi Yisroel and Sara have a very similar story, which they tell in loving detail. There were seven years between when they met and when they married. They were never alone. They never touched, never exchanged a word. All the while, underground, the roots of their love kept growing. This is a story about how love blossoms from noticing the beloved's most unself-conscious acts.

Yisroel: Our story is very unique from a religious and spiritual standpoint.

Sara: I'm just thinking about my mother and everyone else reading this. What should I do? What should I say?

Yisroel: It's very funny because everybody who knows the story, every single person, my parents, her parents and people, they all know a different story. And a lot of pieces of it we've never told them.

Sara: So, basically the beginning is ... When he was 16 Yisroel came to the *Yeshiva* (religious school) in Minnesota. That's where I grew up. And they had a Big Brother program in *Yeshiva* where they set up one of the older

boys to help the younger ones do homework and prepare for *Bar Mitzvah*. Yisroel was set up with my brother who was probably 10 at the time.

Yisroel: Not even.

Sara: Okay, whatever. I was in eighth grade so I originally didn't know Yisroel. My brother would go learn with him once a week and my brother idolized him. He's a great storyteller and my brother loves stories. He would go to sleep every night with a tape next to his bed. He was so excited and always talking about him.

So, eventually my mom decided to invite Yisroel over for a meal on Shabbas and he started coming around and just became part of our family. Sometimes he'd stay for Shabbas and other times just come for a meal.

Usually he'd just pop in, say hello and maybe take the boys to a show or something, or tell them a story.

It also seemed like our families had a lot in common. I had four brothers and he also had four brothers and they were all around the same age. They were all born like one, two, three, four. Also at that time both our brothers were all in elementary school and having a hard time.

	They were all getting "D's" and were really hyperactive. They weren't fitting into the classroom. Both our parents were trying out different forms of Ritalin and so both were going through all these struggles of how to get their boys to stay in class, what to do, and this and that.
Yisroel:	My parents were in Chicago.
Sara:	So, Yisroel decided it would be a great match to introduce both of our parents so that they could network about what to do, what's the best medication. So, our families became really close. Even one year we went to Chicago for *Sukkot* (Jewish Holiday). So, that's where it all began. I mean, we were definitely not in a relationship then at all. We never even spoke to each other.
Yisroel:	The truth is, then, I never even noticed her. I was very studious. I was very... I'd like to tell my version up to here because there were a lot of turns, a lot of things happened. I was very studious. The *Yeshiva* in Minnesota was not exactly the *Yeshiva* of my choice. I'd been accepted to *Yeshiva* in London. I was very excited about going but my mother had a brother who had passed away overseas and I'm the oldest child and she had this thing about me going overseas. It just struck a chord. So even though it wasn't my school of choice, I decided to go to Minnesota for my parents' sake, to give them a little peace of mind. I thought, "I'll make do with whatever it is."
Sara:	At that point, it was more of a *Yeshiva* for boys who were really struggling and a lot of the kids were not very studious. They just wanted to play sports all day and Yisroel was the oddball. I don't think he really had --- you didn't really have friends there.
Yisroel:	It was even worse.
Sara:	He wasn't one of the guys.

Yisroel: It was a small *Yeshiva*, about 50 of us, and there were times when I would be the only one in the classroom.

So, it was a very difficult time and actually my little peace of mind was in the evening when the younger boys would come and I would get a boy to tutor. That was fun. But her brother was really the one. I really connected to him. He would come around even when it wasn't our time to work and we ended up developing this really nice relationship. I was 16 and he was 10.

Sara: Meantime, I had always wanted to go away for high school. I always loved to go away, even to sleep-away camp.

So I convinced my parents to let me go away to high school in Chicago – the big city! And in my second year I actually stayed at his parents' house.

Yisroel: She was staying in my parents' house but by then I was attending Rabbinical school in Miami.

Sara: So we still didn't really have anything to do with each other. I don't think we'd even spoken. We just knew our families were close.

Yisroel: Because of the separation of girls and boys it never even dawned on me to entertain the idea. I was a very serious teenager. I was in rabbinical school seven days a week, 14 hours a day. It's a very, very, very regimented schedule.

Part of the rabbinical training is to be able to master the emotions. Mind over heart. So, I would never, never even allow myself to entertain this idea that there was this girl.

And so, if I had that emotional feeling, I had to be able to master it, to control it. And again, all these boys around me in Minnesota were not exactly so wholesome. I didn't want to be like them. It just struck the wrong chord in my heart to even entertain that idea. Even if I thought about it, I said, "No, no. This thought doesn't exist."

Sara: So, at that same time when I was staying at his parents' house, my brother, whom Yisroel was mentoring, got into a car accident.

He was crossing the street on his way home from school and he was hit by a truck and he was in a coma and was in the hospital and it was big... It was a big deal.

I went home to be with my family. And Yisroel also came to the hospital where my brother was and stayed with him so my parents could, at nighttime, have someone with my brother and they could go to sleep for a couple of hours.

Yisroel: I didn't even think twice. I was in *Yeshiva* in New Jersey at the time. We were still speaking about once a week. I actually had spoken to him the night before. He had just changed schools and he was the best I ever heard.

Sara: Then...

Yisroel: Then one morning somebody runs into the study hall and says do you know this person? And I said, "Absolutely." They said, "He was just hit by a car." And I didn't even – it was a reflex – I got on the phone and the first flight out I went to Minnesota. I stayed there in the hospital for about three and a half weeks until my school started pressuring the local Rabbi in Minnesota.

"What happened to him? Get him back here right away." So finally, I gave in and I went back. Otherwise, I would have stayed longer.

Sara: So, my brother was in a coma for about 14 months, a little over a year. And then my parents eventually were able to transfer him home. They just felt, "Why should he be in the hospital going through all this if we could have nurses at home?" And while he was at home he got some kind of virus and, you know, the immune system is very low in persons in that state. Then he passed away.

[There was a pause, a poignant moment.]

So ... yeah.

Yisroel: It was a very, very difficult time.

[Then there was a much longer pause. The air was quite sad.]

Sara: So, I don't know. We kind of went on. Yisroel went to school in Australia and I actually came to school here in Montreal.

And when I finished high school... His mother is the typical Jewish mother type. Her dream is to get her kids married off. She actually now runs a *Shiddach* (matchmaking) group for moms to network.

Yisroel: My mother thinks that the end of all problems is marriage. Ever since I was two years old, that's all I heard. "When you get married...

When you get married... One day you'll meet her..." That's her whole life. She breathes marriage, breathes it. It's not just that she says it. It's not just that she thinks it. She has marriage bibles of things that she writes, and notes and she's into all these Jewish superstitions.

Sara: So, she had already decided when I was living in her house, that I would be good for her son. She would talk about him to me but she didn't want to get specific. She would say, "One of my kids... one of my kids..." I always knew who she was talking about.

Yisroel: "One of my kids, the one that's in Australia..."

I would call her up. She'd say, "You know, there's a girl staying in my house..."

I didn't know. How would I know which girl is staying in her house?

The most amazing part of it is that we had started, over time and over the years, as the various things happened... I went in for the funeral and again a little later, I stayed almost the entire *Shiva* (the seven day mourning period after a death). I couldn't leave. It was a very, very difficult time.

Slowly my feelings for her started to build but I had no idea what it could be like because we never spoke. I had no idea how she felt about me. I just knew it. I just knew it. And you have to understand, my entire training is mind over heart and this, everything, I mean, I'm very balanced… I mean, this is part of, part of being a Rabbi…and look, I deal with people's emotions all the time… and this just went right through everything.

One time, I was in Morristown in Rabbinical College of America, but I had to go for Shabbas to Crown Heights.

And I knew that weekend was the weekend that all the Chabad high schools went to visit. I was very worried because I really didn't want to see her because I was afraid. I was just afraid.

I got off the subway and I felt that she was a block away. I felt it. I knew it. And sure enough I was walking down the street, I mean, literally we glanced for a second, it was a second. I hadn't seen her in about probably a year.

For a second! For a second, I was walking down the street and I just glanced and we kind of passed an eye. There were thousands of girls, thousands of people. I just was walking the street with my luggage, off the subway, and glanced an eye. We exchanged glances. That was it. That was it. That was our entire interaction for probably a year.

And this whole time… We're talking about how many years? Seven years. And my mother had no idea about this. But from when Sara started living in my parents' house, my mother had this whole thing stirring up anyway.

Sara: As soon as I finished high school, every once in a while I would call his mother up just to wish her Good *Shabbas* and she would say, "Any of your friends getting married?"

Like, "No, I'm 18. Like, "We just finished high school. No."

Yisroel: And it's interesting, it's interesting to find out afterwards that Sara also had that same feeling. And at seven years we both had no idea that each other had any feeling and there was no way to know. There was absolutely no way to know.

Marilyn: Wow, seven years. That's very Biblical.

Sara: So, what happened was this. When I was in my second year out of high school I was working in a school in Philadelphia.

At that same time his mother decided that it was time for him to get married.

So, his mother started looking into all these different prospective girls and I guess she had decided that she should pursue me as well and she called my mother.

And at that point I had seen my friend, who had started dating, going through all this stuff and having a rough time and I thought, "I'll figure out life a little bit before I get married.

I'm not going to rush into this. This is a good opportunity for me to just kind of get my feet wet."

I had already convinced myself that he was not for me. Just because our families are close and I've known him since I was young, it doesn't mean... I wanted... I decided... "I want somebody who's quieter, simpler, somebody who's not so like... I don't know... somebody who's just kind of simple, not too exciting." And I figured this date would be a good closure for this.

I had never ever spoken to boys before. We don't date in a religious world. So I never had a boyfriend. I never really interacted with boys so I figured like it would be a good experience for me to kind of try this out and learn. You know? Going on a date with a boy. Like, Wow!

So, all of a sudden, the night he's supposed to come, I realized this date could possibly work out.

	Like, you know, sometimes you date and then you get engaged and you actually get married. It works. So, I started panicking. I called this woman who was my mentor and I was saying, "I don't know what to do. What should I do? Like, it could really work out. I'm 19 years old. I don't want to get married yet. But I don't know."
Yisroel:	I really did not want to get married. I really had no desire. I had actually planned a trip with my friends to Europe for the summer. I was 22 years old. I was in the middle of writing a book. I was actually going on a lecture tour. I just came back from Sydney and had an amazing experience there. I wanted to just get my bearings and have a good time.

I went home for the holidays. Actually I said, "I'm not going home for the 'holidays', just going home for one day." I knew my mother would start pressuring me. So, I'm home for one day and she says, "Okay so I set you up on a date with Sara."

"Are you serious? What?"

She says "Yeah, I called her mother. She's ready to get married."

And I said to my mother, "Absolutely not. Just, no way, no way."

I was too afraid. His passing was still very, very fresh in my mind. The families are so close; it was just too close to home. What if she doesn't have any feelings for me? It would destroy something that's very, very nice if it doesn't work out. So, I said to my mother, "No."

And she said, "Okay, fine, don't worry. I'll call her up."

So, I went to Boulder, Colorado, for the holidays and my mother calls me up. She says, "I didn't call it off."

"I don't want to deal with this. I am going crazy. Just please call it off. Please call it off. Please call it off."

Mother calls me back. "I bought you a ticket."

You can't fight my mother. She wanted to do what she wanted to do and this is what she did. So, I said, "Okay, fine." I'm just going to do this and whatever happens, happens.

I called her house to set up a date and her mother told me, "Call her cell right now, she's waiting for your phone call." It would be the first time I spoke to her. So I called her and she was very cold on the phone.

Sara: I don't think anyone told me that he was going to be calling. I'm thinking, "Is this how it's supposed to work? Why is he calling me like this in the middle of the grocery store?"

Yisroel: I was told she's waiting for me so I called her up on the phone. I had to tell her where to meet me and she was very cold on the phone. I thought, "Oh no, she's not interested. I just flew from Colorado to Philadelphia for nothing."

The whole thing, my whole life is getting to be thrown up right in front of my face. I said, "It's over." I was already starting to think of doomsday.

Sara: Yeah. So then we went out on Thursday night. We went out on a date and it was really bad in my opinion. I think he thought it was good.

Yisroel: I thought it was good.

Sara: I thought, "He's horrible." He spent a long time talking about everything he did. It was a monologue of your talking about everything you did and like a very guy conversation. I just couldn't wait to leave. But I always felt that when you're meeting someone, you give them a second chance at least. Plus, he was still there. So another night. Saturday night.

Yisroel: Saturday night, Saturday night.

Sara: And it was much better. We had a really good time.

Yisroel: The first date was very tense, very, very tense.

Sara: It was very stiff kind of like...

Yisroel: It was the first time I really had an interaction with speaking to a girl of my age.

Sara: So, then, we decided we would meet in New York and we really had fun, and then he decided to come to Philadelphia to see me.

Yisroel: The second day in New York was very – I don't know, we didn't speak very much. We actually went to The Ritz Carlton. We got drinks in the lobby or something and it was so loud in there. We couldn't hear each other talking so then we went for a walk and I don't know it was just – we were just able to, kind of, you know...

It was very weird because we knew everything about each other but nothing about each other. And it was the strangest thing. We actually started talking like "How is your mother doing?

How are your parents?" Like, it was very difficult because we really knew nothing about each other but everything.

Sara: I don't think the second date was so amazing but the first date was so bad in my opinion and the second one was good enough. We had a decent time. So I thought we'll give it another try.

Yisroel: It's funny because I thought the first day was amazing and the second day was terrible.

Sara: Oh really? So, then we went out in New York and that was great. We had a really, really fun time. We went to ESPN. It's an arcade.

Yisroel: We go to the air hockey and she destroyed me and I was really trying. I was really trying. She just beat me in air hockey.

Sara: Yes, then, in Philadelphia, I think it was a Thursday night and we went for a walk but all of a sudden in the middle of our walk, all of a sudden, he asked me to marry him.

I was, like, "What?" Like, "Where is this coming from?" I always understood that usually there's a stage in between. The *shadchen* (matchmaker) tells you how this person is feeling and you get a heads up. She asks you, "Are you ready to take this to the next level?" And usually you know on this date maybe he'll propose to me. Like, you know. And I was just, like, "What? I don't want to get married now. We've only been dating for two weeks. This is our fourth date," Like, "What? This is too fast."

Yisroel: It was very simple to me. I didn't know what to do next. What am I going to do now? We had a good time. We like each other. Let's get married. What do I know? I'm 22 years old. I never was in a relationship before.

Sara: I was just like, "I don't know what you want me to tell you. I can't just say 'yes' to you just like that, just because you asked me to.

On the other hand, I like you and I don't want to say, 'No, I don't want to marry you.' But I don't *not* want to marry you either." So, I didn't answer him for like a good half hour at least.

Yisroel: We were walking down the street.

Sara: We couldn't find our way back to the car. We were going around in circles. He was so "*not there.*" I said, "Where is the car?" He didn't know. I'm like, "What?"

But eventually I just decided, I don't know, I want to spend the rest of my life with him. Okay, it was maybe a little bit premature but I did not want to say 'No'. So I said 'Yes.'

Yisroel: It was the longest half hour. I just didn't know. Really, I was very innocent.

You know, now, I give all this relationship advice and I've become a little bit of an expert. Thinking back, I cannot believe that I did that.

	I really had no idea what to do. No one ever told me anything. For me it was so simple: Yes or No? Is it going to work or not going to work? Yes, it's working. Okay, Happy Birthday.

Marilyn: **The story you just told took place over seven years. What would be the first moment you first realized each other's potential as a life partner?**

Sara: I think I was in seventh grade and it was Purim time and they had a big carnival and a hayride and he was the storyteller on the hayride. Everyone got to go on the hayride and he was telling a story. It was the first time I ever noticed who he was.

Yisroel: For me, I think that moment happened in the hospital. Through that whole ordeal we were able to see each other.

We were around each other every single day, two people in a relationship, but also not in a relationship, going through all these experiences. We never even spoke. Well, just once. We did speak once.

Sara: But even if you don't speak to somebody, you still get a feeling. I mean, if you know a person for that amount of time, you see them that often, if they're in your house every single week even if you don't speak to them you still know who they are.

Yisroel: What you're asking us to describe was not a moment that words can describe.

I had seen her throughout the whole ordeal and the way she handled it.

I was able to see her in action, the way she was, the way she would be, always. Every single time she walked into the room, my heart sank. That was it.

When I started really thinking about it, there wasn't a doubt on my side.

	But on the other hand, before we went on our first date, we hadn't seen each other for about four years, so I didn't know. Maybe she'd changed. If so, in order to live with that reality, I would have to decide that I'm not going to marry her, and get rid of that thought in my mind. So for two years I was trying to convince myself that she's not for me. She's not for me.
	So when we finally went on that first date I remember that we met in the hotel lobby and when I walked in, I looked and I saw her in the mirror…
Sara:	We both saw each other in the mirror. We didn't see each other for real. I was on one side, he was on the other side and we just kind of looked.
Yisroel:	I saw her. So, for the first time I saw her and all of a sudden… three years… all these emotions… I was ready to melt just right then and there.
Sara:	It was just very emotional.
Yisroel:	I always said, I always said it would make an amazing movie.
Philip:	**And now you've actually been married for six years. How is that changing you?**
Sara:	I feel that when you live with somebody who's so much your other half, it just mirrors who you are. You learn more about yourself. You come face to face with your strengths and your flaws. Maybe I'm more capable than I thought I was.
	I don't know. Little things. For example, in the beginning, when we first got married I was teaching and I had a really hard time doing that because I feel like, "Who am I? Can I handle this classroom?" I guess I always had self-esteem issues. Being married to somebody like Yisroel is empowering, somebody who really sees who you are, and who sees your strength. Because he believes in you, you start to believe in yourself.

Yisroel: I think because our relationship had so much foundation, the past six is more like 60 years. Our relationship has really developed in a very strong, very real way. Personally my work life is very stressful. There are weeks that we probably don't speak but because we have this just-being-next-to-each-other thing, we have this spark, this just-being-in-the-same-room thing, I can feel her, her thoughts and her words without even saying a word. That is part of how our relationship first developed.

I think that having that foundation has really helped develop our relationship in a way that I could not even have imagined. I could never imagine someone just meeting someone, just like that.

And then having a physical relationship or even meeting someone and developing a relationship by words. I think that it would be much harder for us to have that connection if we'd connected that way.

Now my entire life I deal with relationships. I give hundreds of people advice every single day. Over the past year over a thousand different young adults have come through my classes on relationships.

I never even imagined that this would be what I would be doing but it's almost a full time job. Obviously, if you're in your 20s and 30s, what do you care about? Relationship and success. As a Rabbi, that's all I deal with. They call me "The Relationship Guru." I had no idea this is what I was going to be doing. I didn't even know I was good at it.

And who am I? How should I know how to have a relationship? I've never even had anything close to their relationships. I've never had their type of dating. I've never even really dated. I don't have any education besides becoming a Rabbi, with some kind of counseling, some kind of pastoral care training.

Marilyn: **So thousands of people come to you for advice on relationships? What is your secret?**

Yisroel: I have no idea. Sometimes I look around and say, "What the heck are you people doing here? Isn't there a movie on or something?"

When it comes to relationships I feel like an alien coming from a different planet. I understand it in a very different way. So, if I apply my understanding to their world, it's almost like something fresh, a breath of fresh air for them.

I think our relationship has really given me the foundation. Obviously, I've had to learn a lot.

You can see very clearly I made a lot of mistakes in the beginning as far as how I dealt with it. And a lot of people trust me. They come to me and they trust me with their lives, with their relationships.

I think this relationship, especially with our kids, has made me realize that I'm not a selfish person. I grew up in the garbage of this world and in a society that has absolutely no boundaries. I'm 28 years old. Today, I am very much exposed to the society that I live in.

It's all superficial. It's all about "Me! Me!" "What am I going to get? How am I going to do? Is it going to pleasure me?"

My relationship with Sara is the exact opposite. For me, it's not only "give when you want to give"; it's "give when you don't want to give." I think that's a difficult thing living in this world.

I think it's very important because these are the ideals I'm trying to give to these boundary-less young adults.

Philip: **You aren't the first to speak to us of selflessness and boundaries. A lot of Rabbis use the Kabbalah terminology of *Chesed* (generosity) and *Gevurah* (boundaries).**

How do you guys understand yourself in those terms?

Yisroel: I'm definitely the *Chesed* and Sara is the *Gevurah*.

Sara: Oh, that's the way men and women are. Men are *Chesed* and women are *Gevurah*.

Yisroel: I definitely, I definitely have that problem. My greatest challenge is the balance between family responsibility and work and it's a constant battle and it's difficult because everything seems so important. But at the end of the day, who suffers? My family.

And there are so many people that always need help. There's no shortage of work. There's no shortage. We have a very chaotic life and it takes a lot of balance and a lot of work. We have to really work on our relationship because it's so chaotic. Look at how we live.

Sara: Look at all these boxes, someone else's things sitting in our living room. A guest just left our house.

Yisroel: A young boy, he got thrown out of his house. I said, "I don't know what I'm going to do. Leave him homeless?" So, he's just been living in our living room, sleeping on our couch for a while.

Sara: Now, he moved out but his boxes still need to move out.

Philip: You said that women are the ones who set boundaries. Could you say more about how that works for you?

Sara: When I first got married people taught me that marriage is about giving and giving. "Marriage is the first time you really have to give of yourself." And I find it to be the opposite.

Before I was married people would ask for help and I would say, "Yes." I was always available. But once I got married all of a sudden I had needs and if people needed something from me, I had to say, "No."

Yisroel: I think in many ways part of our relationship is that we're community leaders.

	We host a lot of people. I'll tell Sara that there are six people coming on Friday night for dinner and 25 walk in.
Sara:	But I think also we try to put a little bit of a balance in. My mother is kind of a hippy, not very organized, so I grew up in a house where things are flying but I'm trying to figure out how to get more order in my life.
	Like the other week we decided we're not inviting any guests and it would just be our family doing Shabbas.
Yisroel:	And it's very funny. When I walked in alone after shul she gave me this look that said, "No one's with you?"
Sara:	I thought for sure he would say "I know we said just family, but…"
Yisroel:	I had like 10 people there who wanted to come and I said "I'm really sorry." You have no idea how hard it was. I would definitely say that the only time that I have the *Gevurah* is for the relationship. That's the only time.
Marilyn:	**Okay, relationship guru. Can you tell us just one of your secrets about how to have a good relationship?**
Yisroel:	I'll give you a story that just happened. A girl came to me. She had been in many, many relationships and I'd seen her in my classes and I knew that she was not coming to my classes to hear anything I had to say, she was just coming to be around the boys. You know, looking around, "Who can I see? You? Can I see you? Who can I check out?"
	Well, a person has to develop. Finally, one day she goes, "Rabbi I've been in a lot of terrible relationships, can you help me out?"
	I sat down with her and I realized that she was the exact opposite of relationship-phobic. She was desperate. Her standard was just: "Male? He's breathing? Okay. I'll date him." She had become a serial dater only because she had no standards.

And so obviously being a Rabbi, I sat down and I said to her, "Well, I'm going to help you out and I want you to promise me two things. Number one is you will not be in a relationship until I'm finished with you.

No looking at a guy, no trying to find the guy, no nothing. Can you handle that?" She said, "No, Rabbi."

So I said, "Fine. I'm not doing it."

Finally, she comes back to me. "Okay, fine. I'll do it."

I said, "Number two is you have to listen to whatever I say even if you don't like it." And then I said to her that she really has to be able to step out of herself and bring a higher power into her life. She has to do something beyond herself. Give of herself, somewhere, so that it is not for her, so it's not selfish, so she can actually have, what I call in Kabbalah, "The Vessel." You have to have the vessel to get the blessing.

I told her that I was going to work with her for three months. It lasted three weeks. All of a sudden she stopped getting interested in guys. And she had an influx of guys coming to her.

She's going, "Rabbi, I can't handle it anymore. Everybody I see, they want to get involved. What happened?

After the three weeks were over, I said to her, "You know, I think that... I think that you've had a paradigm shift and I'll introduce you to someone." And yesterday she called me up and said, "Rabbi, will you marry us?"

I think for a lot of young adults today it's this paradigm shift that they have to go through. Because most of what they know is from romantic comedies where relationships happen from beginning to end in two hours. That's it.

Sara: I think that people expect that relationships should be really tough. Relationships take a lot of work. But it shouldn't be tough in that way, you know? It shouldn't be painful.

I think, in general, most people's experiences about relationships come with a lot of negativity and baggage.

They have had so many relationships that have not worked out. They just want to protect themselves. Maybe it's refreshing for people to hear that relationship is a positive thing and there is love out there.

Rabbi Bernath is the Rabbi at Chabad NDG, the Chaplain at Concordia University, and Writer and Character Development for Young Avraham Animation. He has also taken his matchmaking abilities online and created a website for Jewish singles to meet. In one year, 2012, according to Chabad, JMontreal.com had facilitated more than 250 introductions. In one year 37 of his introductions have led to marriage.
http://www.jewishmonkland.com/

Rabbi Yisroel and Sara
The Blue Thread in Their Love Story

So Jacob served seven years to get Rachel,
but they seemed to him but a few days
because of the love he had for her
Genesis 29:20

Yisroel and Sara said that after seven years they "saw each other for the first time" and it was an odd thing to say. "First time?" They were around each other for years, often in the same room. Okay, they didn't communicate with each other. They deliberately averted their eyes from each other and certainly never spoke or, God forbid, touched. Yet, despite the discipline, despite the "mind over heart" mantra, they fell in love. Whatever was going on, "It," as Yisroel said, "went right through everything." And whatever *it* was, it created such a powerful foundation for their relationship he felt their six married years together were more like 60.

Something profound was going on during those seven years. They were both aware of it, and whatever it was, it was not the same as "seeing each other." So what was it? It took us a long time to understand because, as Yisroel himself says, this is not the way people today expect relationships to work.

Usually people expect that when they "see" each other for the first and if they are attracted to each other's looks and talk and style, they will be intrigued and they'll begin a courtship dance. It's not until later, when they become a couple and have their struggles, that they start to understand who this person sharing their bed really is. That's the normal sequence today.

With Sara and Yisroel, the whole thing happened in reverse order. First they developed a deep understanding of each other. Then after seven years they "saw" each other – in the mirror, mind you. Then, finally, they spoke. What they fell in love with, even before they "saw" each other, was each other's character. This is the foundation they were speaking of. They knew each other's character before they knew each other's personality.

> Yisroel: We were around each other every single day, ... in the hospital... two people in a relationship, but also not in a relationship, going through all these experiences. We never even spoke.

Yisroel knew her character before he knew she could beat him at Air Hockey. Character is what's there regardless of circumstances or context or mood. Character is what you can comfortably expect of someone over time. It's something that in this day and age we tend to under-value.

In the normal dating world, the one that Yisroel, the Relationship Guru, has never experienced, character doesn't always matter so much. If people are just looking to have a good time, or an adventure, then it's okay for the relationship to end when it's served its purpose. However, in a relationship you want to stay in forever, you need to know what you can count on from the other person. The foundation of an enduring relationship is trust. Character matters.

For us the blue thread was this reminder of the importance of character.

> Yisroel: I was able to see her in action, the way she was, the way she would be, always. Every single time she walked into the room, my heart sank. That was it.

If it's a life partnership, then you know that sooner or later, stuff will happen. "Sooner or later, anything that can go wrong will go wrong." At some gut level, people want to know, "What can I count on from my partner when we are very busy, stressed, grumpy and dealing with some serious challenges? What is the bottom line?"

This is a question about character. And maybe that's why Yisroel, the relationship-guru-who-never-dated, summarized the interview with a story about an enigmatic piece of advice he gave to a young woman about how to find her true love.

Yisroel: *She really has to be able to step out of herself and bring a higher power into her life. She has to do something beyond herself. Give of herself, somewhere, so that it is not for her, so it's not selfish, so she can actually have, what I call in Kabbalah, "The Vessel." You have to have the vessel to get the blessing.*

There is a paradox here, a fine line about the spirit of giving. In order to get the blessing you have to give, but give without expectation. You can't give in order to get. Your generosity has to be a part of your character. If you want your partner to be a certain way, you have to also hold yourself to that standard. Be your best self and you will attract the love you are looking for.

Without being ponderous and preachy, Yisroel and Sara live this with each other, and also teach it to thousands of others.

Chapter Four

How Different Can Two Be and Still Be One?

Reb Haim and Caroline Sherrf

We're very different people, like we're complete opposites. But I think that's what makes it beautiful. You have two people that are the same, one is too many. –Reb Haim

If we didn't have the Torah and all the teachings of marriage, I don't think we'd be married. We had too much to work through. I don't think that we would have stayed married because we were so diametrically opposed in everything. We had that link of the Torah to teach us how. – Caroline

They both remember exactly the same moment in their first encounter, which is unusual, and maybe significant. They first saw each other from opposite ends of a very long hallway. Their eyes met. They both thought, "That's not someone I see every day." This profound attraction happens in an instant across a great distance, a metaphor for their whole relationship.

Theirs is a story about how two strong individuals from very different worlds deal with those differences and create a life together.

Marilyn: **There is often a memory that people hold of the first time they meet each other...**

Caroline: I already know what the story is — but I want to know what my husband has to say; so go ahead, "Charlie."

Haim: Ladies first.

Caroline: It was very simple. I was visiting my sister in Montreal. I was living in New York. I was in acting school and I came to visit her. She was seeing someone seriously and doing *T'shuvah* (when a secular Jew embraces Orthodox Judaism). She invited me to her future fiancé's parents' home. I was in the kitchen. I glanced down this long hallway and somebody walks in, pauses and looks around.

I am from New York and he was very well dressed and so that caught my eye. He had this short beard. We clicked with our eyes first.

He was gorgeous so, of course, my attention was riveted. But being 20, I just proceeded to ignore him because I was being 20 years old. I just flirted with my eyes a little bit. But that was it. It was attraction from the beginning.

I wasn't a 35-year-old woman or 40-year-old woman with maybe a few relationships behind me. It was just an extremely strong attraction to him and I just made sure I was sitting close to him at the table so I could keep looking, keep assessing. But it was such a strong pull towards this man. So it was really with the eyes, the eyes first.

Haim: I got this invitation for Shabbas lunch. When I entered the house, I saw across the hallway— it's a long hallway, very long hallway—and I see this beautiful woman sitting on the chair and I say, "This is something that's worth examining closer."

So I started walking towards the attraction. I was a little hesitant because I realized she wasn't religious. I was already quite religious. But I always followed my instinct in life and, fortunately, I was never wrong. And I said, "I'm gonna explore this one."

And, of course, over lunch, even though she was ignoring me, I was experienced enough to know that she was interested. So I went to Ephraim, who was to be the husband of Caroline's sister, and I said to him "I'm gonna make specially tonight a *Malevah Malka* (special end-of-Sabbath meal) and you better make sure she comes."

So we had lunch, we had fun and then I went home and I prepared right away the *Malevah Malka*. And she came in and it was beautiful. We started talking and I really ignored everybody else. And we just talked, talked, talked and for the next two weeks we were talking and talking. I was more and more attracted.

And then we started making plans. I think it was after two weeks that I proposed.

Caroline: Ten days.

Haim: Ten days.

Caroline: I did accept but I told him I need to go study. I was very new to the religion so I went for a few months to a seminary.

And another reason I emphasized the way that my husband looked was because he used to sport two earrings and a ponytail and if I had seen that I would've run in the other direction.

So it was very good that he had a suit on... not the whole biker look. But, you know, he is an artist.

Haim:	Actually, the Shabbas after that, again, I made such a beautiful Shabbas. We were reading poetry the whole Shabbas for each other and I cooked the whole meal.
Caroline:	We were pretty much inseparable. I would go to my sister's house and we would just sit outside as long as possible before we'd go in.
	Once it was raining, it was just so cozy, just sitting in his very tiny little car and getting to know each other.
	If my daughter would do that, I'd have a fit, an absolute fit. It's not the religious way, not the proper way to choose a spouse and life-mate.
Marilyn:	**Were you expecting someone to show up in your life at that time? Were you looking for something?**
Caroline:	Well, there's a lot of pressure in Manhattan to be perfectly groomed and to be perfectly slim, perfectly educated, to be *au courant* with all the events, and see every show and hear every musician and be at every gallery opening. It's kind of an empty pressure because people want to excel, which I admire—I admire the drive and the striving for excellence—but I didn't find any spirituality there. I always thought something was wrong, something was missing.
Haim:	I wasn't expecting to meet anyone at Shabbas, definitely. But I was ready. I was actually exploring a few options at the time. Before I was religious, I was very wild and I toured the world and I explored. I went through Europe with a backpack after the army.
	I had traveled extensively and I said to myself now I'm ready for a family, for stepping back and giving all to my children and my wife. I just wanted to make sure I had the right partner.

I could see the potential in Caroline right away. "She probably is the one," I thought. This is what I wanted, to build my family and my children. And I wanted to have a big family and as many children as my wife and I can afford. To me it's just more joy. It was always my dream to have my own tribe.

When you have faith and you have trust in God, then God provides; if you think it's in your hands, then God will leave it in your hands.

Marilyn: **You're so different. What kinds of adjustments did you have to make to be together?**

Caroline: We were very fortunate – We didn't know each other very well at all when we got married. And everything was different, culturally and geographically and language and everything. The food...everything was different. It was an adjustment, definitely...

We have tons of adjustment stories!

I grew up in New York City where people do not come to the door without a gold-plated invitation. Dinner parties are catered. And in New York City you're always going out. My mother was a single mother. She was going on dates. I was going on dates. My sister was going on dates.

His mother was completely different. They were observant, very traditional Sephardic Jews, and they had an open home, lots of people showing up and sleeping over. And it wasn't a large home.

My husband loves people. I like my privacy. Now we always have people living with us. So that is a big compromise. But now, I'm starting to enjoy it, especially because my darling husband has bought me a lot of help. I have someone who takes over Friday night.

We say in Judaism that another person's physical needs are our spirituality. So it's very good for one's self-development to give to others. But it's nice not to be the waitress and to enjoy my guests. If you've ever worked in a kitchen or waitressing in a restaurant with a lot of screaming and things clattering and wanting everything to be perfect for the guests, you know. That was a big adjustment, definitely.

Haim: My adjustment? Well, I think, as an Israeli, maybe I'll throw in also *Sephardic* (meaning Jews of North Africa and Spanish, rather than Eastern European, descent), the man tends to be quite dominant and selfish.

For some reason, I don't know why, culture just made it this way. One thing I will thank my wife greatly for is that she taught me how to see other ways and accept them.

Caroline: It's been like water on a stone. He thinks he's stubborn but I'm like an immovable object.

Haim: Well, it's just interesting how through the years, in quite a smart way, my wife pretty much got me to do anything she wants.

Here's an example. I love having guests. My greatest pleasure is Shabbas, especially Friday night. And I like to enjoy that day. For me it's special. To sit at the table with no guests, it's a depression for me. But for my wife it's hard.

So I said to her: "Let's work it out. How can I make it easier for you? Don't do anything. Let me buy all the food. Let me get maids, whatever you need just to make it easier for you." I think she was trying to be considerate because she didn't want to spend the money.

She thought I expected her to do everything, which was overwhelming. Plus, we have eight kids so it's a very overwhelming task. But when she realized that I really meant it and it was okay to spend the money, then things became easier for all of us.

So we learned to adjust through the years with this relationship. We're very different people, like we're complete opposites. But I think that's what makes it beautiful. You have two people that are the same, one is too many.

Philip: **It's one thing to see those differences the first time you meet and then a very different thing to start to have to live with them. Could you give us a story about when you first started to understand the challenges?**

Caroline: For our honeymoon, we go and spend three weeks in the Negev in Israel. "Honeymoon" is not even the right description of the trip that we took. It was more like doing charity work.

It's boiling hot, it's July, and I knew I was pregnant. I could feel something, because I was very irritable and I'm usually pretty even-tempered. It was boiling hot and while he's speaking Hebrew to the mayors of all these little towns I sat in offices drumming my fingers. It's not what I expect for a honeymoon. I'm an American girl. And I didn't have the communication skills to say, "Hey, I want to go to a hotel with a pool and be alone!"

Then a busload of people show up. Like, he got all the buses and all the halls and all the activities set up. He did a great thing. And then where do we stay? Oh my gosh, do you know what a *Peneem Meenya* is?

It's a boarding school in Israel. This is not the posh East Coast boarding school. This is so primitive. There are holes in the walls with birds flying in and out. You walk in and you are just hit by the spray that they had just done for cockroaches. There are dirty mattresses on the floor, urine-soaked mattresses.

And then someone gives me what can only be called a rag for a blanket and I said, "That's it! Goodbye! I'm going home to your mother. I'll see you in Haifa when you're finished with all your business!" And that was it.

So I always told him "You owe me a honeymoon."

And, by the way, we're going for our first vacation together ever in March to Barbados. So we waited 21 years but now I'm getting to go!

Marilyn: **So how did the relationship change you? What kind of adjustments did you have to make?**

Caroline: I didn't know what I wanted. Because of both my life experience and his coming from the culture that he did, he expected to be boss. Not that he was a despot or anything mean, but I would just naturally fall in with whatever his desires were or his wishes.

He's almost ten years older than I am. At that time that was a big age difference. I had to grow up also. I didn't make any demands, really, like, "Help me with the kids." I just did everything and he was busy helping everyone else.

So later, as I started to discover what I wanted, who I was, then he had to adjust.

Like he says he's unselfish. He sees a need and to him, it's like there's a fire raging. Sometimes I would joke to people I'm Lois Lane.

This person doesn't have a job. These people, they just came in and they don't have a place to stay. This family's being evicted; I have to go collect money for them. And he'll do it all.

But I wouldn't want to be married to someone who wasn't like that.

I didn't realize that I have to ask. I just assumed that he should know. I mean he's so intuitive and he's helping everyone else and I'm thinking, "Wait, hello, I'm your wife! I'm number one, actually. I have needs, I need you to come, I need you to be here for the kids, I'm tired, take the baby."

But I guess he thought that I was so strong.

When I had my sixth child we were having 40 guests at the time, 40 every Shabbat, plus I was going to school part time so I said "That's it, I want full time help."

He says, "Okay, that's a good idea."

"What?" *(Chuckle)*

So I needed to grow up. So I started to make these kinds of demands—no, "requests," not "demands"—and then, because I started to ask, then he started to be more intuitive. Then he would realize without my asking "She needs this; she needs that."

It just obviously builds love. I sometimes tell girls who are newly married and who have certain frustrations and I say "You're not making enough demands.

The whole thing for a man is to grow through marriage." By having your needs fulfilled, you're causing your husband to grow. In Judaism, we say, "The more you give to someone; the more you love them," and if you're not making any demands, then you're not even building love in your husband.

I always say "It's really hard to be a Jewish man." It's very difficult, and it's not under the *chuppah* (marriage canopy) that he suddenly becomes a *tzaddik* (righteous man) and knows "I have to do this for my wife and this and this." It's only as he lives with her and he realizes.

	I remember a few years ago you wrote me such a beautiful love letter: "I was a wild one but you tamed me and you taught me."
Haim:	One of the big adjustments was the language. In Israel, there are no smooth corners. Language is direct, short and the facial expressions suggest almost hostility. So I would be talking to my wife that way and she thinks that I'm angry with her or I'm being so bossy and I wasn't. That was just the way I grew up. So it took her time to realize that it was just a style. And it took me time to soften. So somewhere we met in the middle.
Caroline:	He's the most tenderhearted guy you can imagine but the way he would speak sometimes, I couldn't bear to hear that. I wanted everything to be very sweet, and super gentle, even the criticism. I would say "Just tell me in the sweetest, nicest way because I'm very fragile and I want to hear it in the most tenderhearted way."

He really softened, enormously. He went all the way to my side, I would say.

True closeness comes in a marriage in true compromise.

You can see your spouse behaving a certain way over and over again, but when you really understand them, who the person is, then you build that caring and the trust.

It took me a long time, almost 15 years, to figure it out. I don't remember the exact moment but I remember him coming in and being upset, and me stepping out of my usual self and coming to him, embracing him, and saying, "What's going on; what's wrong?" I remember him with the tension just deflating like a balloon, just relaxing in my arms, just opening up and realizing it's not something he has to keep to himself and be strong.

Also I remember coming in one day. Someone had really done the dirty on him, had really been awful, really awful, and so he was so down about it. So I said, like, "That's it. I spit on them." And I started grinding my heel on the ground and saying, "This is what we're going to do with them," and acting really silly about it, and his mouth started quivering in the corner and then he started laughing. And that was it. "We're making a voodoo doll!" I said. "Whatever it takes."

And he smiled...I finally knew who he was. I knew that that wasn't him.

For me, I had to learn to not be so easily hurt and easily overcome, to know that he's reacting to something external, to say to myself, "Hey you know it's not a personal thing."

Haim: A few days ago, you know, I was sort of exhausted and a little bit stressed because there's a lot of pressure on me. I look at my wife and I see that she's sad too. I said to her, "Why do you feel like that?"

And she said, "Because you're so stressed."

And so I said to her, "That's not your job," I said, "Everything is okay. "You don't need to be in my mood to make me feel better. You be cheerful and that's a source of strength for me."

Philip: **So you've really done a lot of work learning to know and appreciate each other and your differences. What's the growing edge for you now? What's a current issue in your relationship?**

Caroline: My husband had to learn that when one person wants to do this and another person wants to do that, it's not bad or good. It's just what I want to do. It has as much validity as what he wants to do.

His idea of relaxing is to make a meal and play guitar and then sit and talk. But my idea, growing up in New York, was that you did things. You went out. You experienced. You went out to dinner and someone cooked and then you discuss what you just experienced.

The way I grew up everybody was in the gym, the ballet class, the yoga studio.

And then, finally, he realized that I wanted that. He was, like, "Well, okay do it, but you know that it's going to be inconvenient to me."

I'm like, "Inconvenient? What?" I mean he didn't say it in those words. He never said that. But in essence that was what it was.

For me, I need my free time. He wanted me with him all the time, all the time. I said, "There is Separate Time in a relationship."

So my way was... "Okay. I'm going to continue doing what I'm going to do, and he's going to react. But I'm just going to keep doing it.

That's because I'm not going to change something that's perfectly reasonable."

Haim: What's reasonable is what works in a relationship, not what makes sense.

I mean my wife's working-out pattern. I encourage her to work-out for many reasons. First, it puts her in a good mood, always. Second, she looks good, which I benefit from. I want her to be healthy and I want her to be happy but it's just the time that it worked for her was inconvenient to me.

Caroline: I think we're still working on this one.

Haim: Yeah. Well, let me finish. First of all, she has to do her work-out in a very confined area and it's hard for her to move around. So we have to move the couch. It's a big couch and this couch blocks the whole entrance. It's an expensive couch that's been dragged all over the place.

So I think, "My poor wife, she's not at the Y where she would be more comfortable in an open area with the right equipment. She's being modest and she's being frugal because she does not have to pay any membership and it's not easy. So now I learn to go around the couch, to squeeze my way.

The one thing I told her is, *Meretz Ha Shem* (God Willing), when we build a new home which I hope we will do, she's going to get her master room with all the mats and the bar and the mirrors, everything she needs. I would love to build it because I want her to be happy. What I do now is I try to be out of the house when exercise happens, and I think she tries to do it when I'm not in the house.

Caroline: I'll tell you, from a spiritual standpoint, I really feel that I don't think we're going to get a new house until this issue is resolved because I think that...

Haim: Don't say that. The angels are listening.

Caroline: I think that my husband is amazing because it's hard for someone who is a masterful man and a man's man to hear criticism.

That's one thing. But to hear it from me, and in front of other people, it's not so easy.

I mean I don't have to be spiritual and go to shul three times a day to know that it's "People before things." If you see how small the house is when he comes in... there's two couches pulled out and all the chairs pulled out and you do have to go through like a maze. But I'm thinking "So what? So squeeze through a maze for five minutes. What's the big deal?"

We're still working on this.

	I don't think I'm a very high maintenance person. I'm just saying these are my few hours. He's come a long way because for him he wants everything to be a certain way and I would say that's controlling.
	So it's hard for my husband, it's hard. It's very hard but he's still working on it.
	I remember a couple of months ago he started telling me, "Gosh, I don't know how you put up with me. I am arrogant and macho and bossy." Then he's looking at me at the corner of his eyes and I'm smiling. As if I'm going to stop him?!
Haim	Well, I think that God puts a test in people's way.
Caroline:	Like I'm not a *Balabusta* (traditional Jewish homemaker).
	I grew up, we were two girls and my mother and a cleaning lady who came three times a week. I'm not a great housekeeper.
	So that was a compromise for him to come home and have to step over things and not having everything in order and it's very hard for him.
	I know it's hard for him. He would love to come home and it's a nice tranquil oasis but it's very rarely like that. That's even with help. I have full-time help now. Because we have a large family and I'm not the most organized person.
	So I'm just saying it has to be completely resolved, spiritually. So he has to compromise. It's spiritual work to compromise and overcome and fix our character traits. We do that for our spouse. That's the greatest test, for our spouse to fix our character traits.
Haim:	You know what? My wife is very intelligent, very observant and even when she's not right, she's right. If she has understood something and it's for her, then I have to accept that maybe I need to adjust to that.

	But if it's something that doesn't work for me, then I will let her know. I think I'm pretty direct. Only the difference is the way I used to say things. Before, the way I talked could be more direct and sound maybe more harsh. Now maybe it's more considerate and softer.
Caroline:	He's very considerate. He really is.
Haim:	It's always the same message just packed differently.
Caroline:	I also have to say that my husband has done most of the adjusting in the marriage. I really feel that.
	He really had to, because he's had to change things that were part of his personality, part of his essence, and I don't feel like I had to do that so much. Even if I had to make a few changes in my lifestyle... but he really... he's done it. I don't know too many people who can do that. I really don't.
Haim:	It's interesting. I have friends where the husband is Israeli and the wife is American or Canadian and then I look at the husband, I almost see myself years before, and it's so terrible. I get a flavor of the selfish man just thinking of himself.
Caroline:	I have an *Ashkenazi* friend (Eastern European Jew) and she was saying something negative about my husband and I responded, "My husband is *Sephardic.* It's different for you. You started in a matriarchal house with a certain kind of man raised in a matriarchal house and you're matriarchal in your house."
Haim:	They have an *Ashkenazi* house.
Caroline:	*Ashkenazi.* And you see her in a temper slamming around in the kitchen and all irritated. Then her husband will start cracking jokes to cajole her out of her temper. But he is just calm.

I thought of my husband and I felt this wellspring of love flowing from him. He's such a good man. People are not willing to do that work in a relationship. I've seen people saying "I'm not going to change" and "I'm not getting my needs met." And yet Haim is there and he is doing and growing.

And that's besides all the other things that I got right away. He's loyal, he's like a rock, he's dependable. And he is strong. I can lean on him. And I could come to him.

Marilyn: **Can you name what is the spiritual edge in your relationship? Were there places that, maybe you wouldn't have gone on your own?**

Caroline: I would never have met so many amazing people.

It's also the essence of spirituality to be thinking about the other and doing for the other. And I've come to this because I live with my husband and that's what his life is about.

I mean growing up, the way I grew up in Manhattan, people are so much about self-development but in a selfish way. It's "I'm going to improve myself, improve myself." But it's just like a shell. It's like a beautiful statue. Where's the inner? The innerness?

So, because of staying married, when... You know I'm sure both of us went through times when, "I don't want to be married. I'd rather be by myself" or "It's not worth it."

But just staying married and just staying in the process, I saw his example. I just didn't grow up like that. I didn't grow up seeing someone who wants to raise money for people to help them. He helps physically. I mean he'll schlep. He'll find people jobs. He'll bring people together and facilitate marriages. I mean we've all been sleeping on the floor while we've had guests filling up our entire house.

Sometimes the judgments can come about other people, but helping the person anyway is what matters. My husband is like, "They need help. It doesn't matter anything about them. Their story doesn't matter. They need help and how can we not help them?"

We had this one family who stayed with us for a few months, quite a few months. And they definitely wrecked our house up. I mean our piano had to be gotten rid of. The kids were writing on some of his paintings! But I said to my husband and I really meant it, "I'm glad we don't have a house like A and B and C of our friends because then we couldn't do this mitzvah.

We'd be tearing our hair out." It was already a little bit. You know I had a few moments where finally I asked him, "Can we really do this mitzvah?" And he didn't have to think about it. "Of course, they need to be here." And so that's how he is about helping people. Only exhaustion stops him, only exhaustion.

Haim: I do a lot of marriage counseling and I speak to a lot of couples. I think that's also taught me a lot about my own relationship. I give a lot of credit to my wife because she wasn't used to all this hospitality. Yet she does it. And I think she will get a lot of credit for that. And she doesn't do it because she loves doing it; she does it because it needs to be done. I think this is true unselfishness.

When you do something and you enjoy doing it, it's almost like you're doing it for yourself. I think it was in our relationship that this was where I had to work on my own selfishness, where I had to do things where it's not convenient. That's what helped me to grow. That's the true kindness, *Chesed*, where it's not comfortable to be done.

Philip: **Your home is so often filled with guests. Service to others is important. But how do you make times for just you two, for each other?**

Haim: I think I learned through the years to find privacy in the crowd.

Like I'm almost romancing with my wife within the crowd. We have a large table. We sit next to each other. We're looking at each other. Sometimes we touch each other under the table. So we have our almost privacy within the crowd. We learn to almost ignore everybody and yet to be there.

Caroline: But we definitely have our alone time. As much as I say we didn't have a honeymoon, we definitely manage to carve that time and if we lose some sleep we lose some sleep.

But, you know, finally, everyone is in bed and our bedroom door closes and we are alone, and the intimacy is there, and our deepest, sweetest and most tender conversations are at those times. I can come to my husband.

Sometimes he'll come back home and everyone has gotten off to school and he'll come and he'll sit with me and we'll have some coffee or some oatmeal or something and we have a very good conversation and share everything.

Haim: Relationship could be done in a most beautiful way or it could be very dirty. It's how you treat it. I think that this is something that Judaism taught me a lot.

The real relationship comes much before. It's how to talk to your wife, how to please her, how to treat her. It's only then that you're together physically and that's maybe the epitome of that moment of that relationship.

Caroline: If we didn't have the Torah and all the teachings of marriage, I don't think we'd be married. We had too much to work through. I don't think that we would have stayed married because we were so diametrically opposed in everything. We had that link of the Torah to teach us how.

I consider myself a Jewish religious feminist. This means I want my husband to follow exactly what it says in the Torah about how to treat a woman. Sometimes I think that women's expectations are actually too low in a secular world, too low about what a man should do.

The beginning point is putting a ring on a woman's finger, the minimum is putting a ring on and committing...that's just the beginning. I expect to get happier and happier every year and I am. I am happier all the time because he is a better and better husband.

Intimacy is so important. I mean the Torah says a husband should make his wife happy.

He's a wonderful husband and when we're in each other's arms and we're talking, we have that closeness, we definitely do. I really cherish that because it builds intimacy. I mean I had a teacher and she's saying the minimal time that you should be intimate, by the way, minimum, by the Torah, is twice a week when you're able to be together. She said because this is the only relationship where you have this act, where you have this. And she says *that* should be the *Shema* (the principle daily prayer) between the husband and wife.

You should only be thinking of each other, you know, and it's so beautiful. And when someone gives to you so much and when it make you feel so good in there, and also when they delay their own pleasure and they put themselves to the side to give to you, because women generally need a little bit more than men. Like we say in the Torah, "Her pleasure is his pleasure."

	I mean besides the physical closeness and all the chemicals and hormones that are released, the fact that someone is so loving to you and giving, of course, builds so much intimacy and it's one of those beautiful parts of the marriage. It really is.
Haim:	There's something I read once about someone who wants to have beautiful children and holy children so they think about this righteous person or that righteous person and it always, I'm sorry to say, it turns me off. Why would I want to think about someone else if I have my wife to think about? Finally I found once a scripture that said that actually the highest *Kavana*, the highest intention, for having pure children and good children are actually thinking about your wife. It's only when you cannot think about your wife that you start thinking about these other righteous people. Your wife is the best thing to think about.
	My wife and I, we share the same dreams. It's like we know we're together, we're a family. We drink together and talk about plans. We talk about the future and we know that we're sharing the same dreams.
	We're almost one. It's very beautiful.

Reb Haim is a chaplain and artist. His art may be seen at **http://www.sherrf.com/**

Reb Haim and Caroline
The Blue Thread in Their Love Story

"Shema Yisroel, Adonai Elohenu Adonai Echad."
"Listen all of you who wrestle with God.
All the different Faces Of God;
They are all One."
(An interpretive translation of the Central Prayer in Jewish Liturgy)

Shared Love has so many faces. The temptation is to say that *this* is the one true face of our marriage but not *that*. It's an easy mistake to make. When we're in one of those moments, a particularly wonderful one, or a particularly awful one, it does feel like that single moment is the Whole Truth about the Relationship.

When love is authentic, partners visit many emotional places, some of great harmony, some of dissonance and tension. And, the more different the partners are, the greater the potential for dissonance. However, all those moments are sacred, all part of the One. This is the blue thread. This is what we need to remember.

This blue thread is the principle of the Shema applied locally: "You who wrestle with your relationship remember that all the different phases of that relationship, harmonious and contentious, are all part of the One." This is a disciplined perspective, a spiritual practice.

For us, the conversation with Haim and Caroline was a study in how to live from that perspective. They come from such different worlds. Their differences could be an impossible obstacle for some. Not for them. For them, dealing with differences is part of their spiritual work. The bigger the differences, the more they get to do.

> Caroline: *It's spiritual work to compromise and overcome and fix our character traits. We do that for our spouse. That's the greatest test, for our spouse to fix our character traits. True closeness comes in a marriage in true compromise.*

"True compromise." This is a very common challenge in a relationship. Who has to do the compromising? How much do they have to do? Can one compromise too much? When does one need to say, "This is me, who I am. I can't change"? When to say, "I will change to whatever you want"? Couples are always walking a path between two slippery slopes, between being too rigid and too accommodating. We learned so much from how Caroline and Haim walk that path, and also from how their understanding of True Compromise evolved over their decades together.

Caroline started out doing most of the adjusting. As a young wife in a new culture and a new spiritual practice she believed in being accommodating and not making demands.

Caroline: *I didn't make any demands... I just did everything... We say in Judaism that another person's physical needs are our spirituality. So it's very good for one's self-development to give to others.*

After their sixth child she saw that the situation was much more complex.

Caroline: *I needed to grow up. I started to make demands --- no, "requests," not "demands." Then, because I started to ask, then he started to be more intuitive. Then he would realize without my asking, "She needs this; she needs that." It just obviously builds love.*

Haim: *I think it was in our relationship that this was where I had to work on my own selfishness, where I had to do things where it's not convenient. That's what helped me to grow.*

Caroline: *I sometimes tell girls who are newly married and who have certain frustrations and I say, "You're not making enough demands.*

The whole thing for a man is to grow through marriage." By having your needs fulfilled, you're causing your husband to grow.

This claim, that making demands of your partner is helping him to grow is radical. It goes against much relationship advice. There are many teachers who say, "Don't try to change your partner. Change yourself."

But this couple is advocating that it's a good thing, even a spiritual gift, for a partner to make demands and requests. This helps the other to grow.

Still, this is not a license to nag. And here is the fine line, the way they do it. We see this most clearly in their discussions and their adjustment stories. Neither of them backs down.

Caroline: *It's been like water on a stone. He thinks he's stubborn but I'm like an immovable object.*

At the same time they are so gentle and kind with each other. Haim constantly acknowledges how much he appreciates the changes she's asked for, and how much he appreciates the way he has changed as a result. *"I was a wild man and she tamed me."* At the same time Caroline constantly says how much she admires and appreciates him. There is this amazing combination of love and persistence.

Caroline says that the greatest reminder of their unity, are all those moments of profound intimacy which they share in private with each other, those times at night, when they are in bed, alone, talking and making love.

Haim: *I like the fact that we are sharing the same dreams. It's like we know we're together, we're a family. We're almost One.*

Caroline: *He's a wonderful husband and we're in each other's arms and we're talking and we have that closeness. ... I really cherish that. This is the only relationship where you have this act... That should be the Shema (the principle daily prayer) between the husband and wife.*

For her, this is their *Shema*, their "daily prayer," their reminder of the essential unity of everything that has happened between them and around them in the life they are building. Then their differences become gifts.

Chapter Five

Do Not Awaken Love till it is Ripe

Rabbi Shefa Gold and Rachmiel O'Regan, M.A.

As in the Song of Songs, that's how I want to live, with that much impeccability... "Then streams come forth from Eden toward the Garden"... And when I'm not there, then it's really my own work to reconnect. – Rachmiel

I see my main practice as taking every moment of my life and feeling myself addressed by God, the Beloved, and also addressing God. Then I can be with Rachmiel from the overflow of that relationship instead of coming to him with my neediness, I'm coming to him with the fullness of this love that I have for God's Reality. So Rachmiel then gets the benefit of me being in love with Life. – Rabbi Shefa

In Shefa's translation of the Song of Songs, *"In the Fever of Love,"* this phrase, *"Swear to me, that you will not awaken love till it is ripe.",* occurs over and over. What is it saying about love?

Is it about when to be apart and when to be close?

Is it about savoring the yearning?

Is it an erotic teaching about love-making?

Is it, maybe, advice for people who are single at midlife, to not give up hope?

Is it about patience and timing?

How long one might have to wait for the chance to live like the lovers in the Song of Songs?

Shefa and Rachmiel's interview touches on all these questions as they share their stories about their late-in-life initiation onto the path of love.

Marilyn:	**Share with us your memory of the moment when you first realized that this person was going to be a significant person in your life.**
Shefa:	I knew right away; he took a few months.
Rachmiel:	I was a little slower.
Shefa:	After our first date, our first time alone together in late December, I went to this hot spring resort and got a massage. I lay on the table and the masseur put his hands on me and immediately this great presence came into the room who identified himself as Eliahu.

And he said to me, "You're about to step onto a path because a new door is opening for you in your life. It has to do with how energy manifests in your life. Up until this moment you've been on the path of fission. Fission is a kind of a breaking of the heart and out of that breaking, yearning is manifested from your heart, and that yearning moves you towards God."

That's the path I had been on, building energy in hearts through the breaking of hearts.

"But," he said, "There's a new door opening and it's a door to the path of fusion which is a different way for energy to be created."

And Eliahu said, "You have a choice now whether you want to walk through this door. If you don't, then the path that you're on will destroy you. But it's your choice."

So immediately at that moment Rachmiel's face appeared in my mind and I knew that he had been sent to me to be my partner on the path of fusion. So it was very clear that there was some shift in my heart, where I would walk now. I think that was my moment of knowing. |
| Rachmiel: | At the end of December of '99. |
| Shefa: | Yeah. And then we met and it was the time of the New Year, of the New Millennium. |

For about a month before I met Rachmiel I had been doing some searching inside my heart and found a kind of hopelessness about relationships.

I had been married two times before. I'd been told by astrologers that nobody could possibly manage to be my partner.

Rachmiel: One in a million.

Shefa: It's one in a million, right? Really, there was this sense that I didn't want to enter the New Millennium carrying this burden. So I did a practice for a month that was all about creating hopefulness in my heart.

I was taking a phrase from the liturgy and creating a chant from it that was all about hope. And at the end of the month of doing that, there was this whole kind of a shift. That's when I met Rachmiel.

So on New Year's Eve, we did a little drumming at a friend's place and then we came back around 11:30 at night and set up my meditation room like the Tree of Life with candles at each of the *Sefirot* (kabbalistic mystical spheres), and also at *Keter* (the crowning sphere). There was a big window that looked out over the valley, a very beautiful, beautiful view, and we sat and looked out at the valley. And at the stroke of midnight, as we entered into the New Millennium, I said, "Let's do a kissing meditation," where we create energy in the kiss and send it out to the world.

It was going to benefit the whole world and not just ourselves, whatever love was between us was going to be sent out to the world. So there was a bursting out of our relationship.

Rachmiel: That was wonderful. I remember.

Shefa: And then the next day, I called up all my friends and said, "This is it. I met him. This is it." But...

Rachmiel: But it took me a few more months to know.

	We had met briefly in October. And I was the first local person that she met.
Shefa:	Because I just moved here.
Rachmiel:	And she said, "Well, why don't you show me around the valley?" And I said, "I'd love to. When do you want to get together?" And she flipped through a little calendar in her book. This is October. I'm a local guy and, I'm thinking next week. She said, "How does December 20th work for you?" And I said, "What?"
Shefa:	I had a very busy schedule.
Rachmiel:	So that gave me a clue right away. But in the meantime, while we're waiting, right after my birthday, November 18th, we happened to be in the same local restaurant together.
Shefa:	Actually Rachmiel was with another woman. I was with another man eating dinner and we saw each other across the crowded room.
Rachmiel:	I went, "Oh, that's the woman I just met. Oh, Shefa."
Shefa:	So we just kind of floated towards one another and there was this big – I don't know – a very powerful hug that happened.
Rachmiel:	It was the first hug. We had never even hugged before.
Shefa:	And we didn't even know how that happened. And I came back to the table and the guy I was with said, "Who was that who just mauled you?"
Rachmiel:	And my friend and I, we weren't in a relationship, just really good friends, but she said, "Wow, who is she? Who is that?" And I said, "Wow, I don't know, I was just going to go say hello to her and then we were just hugging."
Shefa:	Just pulled into a vortex. It was just a startling kind of moment. We didn't know what that was about.

Rachmiel:	Totally mutual, like, "Wow!" and totally unexpected. So that was a clue. But then it was another month before we actually got together.
Shefa:	Then on New Year's Eve, it was Shabbat. Rachmiel had never experienced Shabbat and when I explained it to him, he just said, "Wow, I've been looking for this my whole life."
Rachmiel:	Shabbat is a 25 hour sacred practice.
Shefa:	So I always say that he fell in love with Shabbat before he fell in love with me. He's a real Shabbat lover. And he keeps me to it. It's very important to him. Shabbat is like a main practice of our relationship. I can get somewhat obsessive about my work and he can remind me that Shabbat is about putting it all down and being together. Every Shabbat we get married again.
Rachmiel:	Yeah. After our hand washing, we do the rings and ask each other.
Shefa:	When Rachmiel really fell in love with Shabbat, I could see how important it could be for our relationship. But I'm only home half the time. So it's very precious when I am home and we can do Shabbat together.
Rachmiel:	And when Shefa is gone, I still do Shabbat, light candles and the whole thing. Because I came into Judaism from a pagan community, reclaiming the tradition of Wikka with Starhawk and the gang which was very aligned with Jewish renewal principles. And I was all excited to have a weekly ritual to do with Shefa. There are not a lot of guys like me, but there are a percentage of us, ritual lovers, and goddess lovers and all that. Part of my spiritual belief stems from the Green Man, the god from Europe and Ireland who was the Good Steward for the Goddess's creation.

	He would help the trees and the plants grow and protect the animals and take care of them.
	The Good Steward. I mean, that's where husbandry, the word, actually, came from.
	I really see myself as the Green Man to Shefa as the goddess.
Marilyn:	**So you had already done a lot of inner work. Did you ever wonder whether you'd find someone who could match you in that way?**
Rachmiel:	A few weeks before we met, which would be three months before we started dating, I had gone to a psychic and got a reading, and the psychic said to me, "You've done a lot of work on yourself, I can really see that." And then, in my frustration, I said, "I've done all this work on myself and now I'm wondering what woman wants to be with me. I'm this weird guy who wants to work on his stuff."
	And she said, "No. No. There's a smaller percentage of available partners, but there is a partner for you. In fact, I see one coming."
	So, I guess, there was a little bit of openness to it in the midst of my hopelessness also.
	So I knew it was very special at the very beginning when we met and hugged in the restaurant. I can still feel it. We were in the Star Trek beam.
	Then I guess it was sometime later, in March 2000. We were in a hot tub together and what I heard was, "Do you want to move in and live together?" and I missed the first part of what she was saying.
Shefa:	Really what I was saying was, "Why don't we start *talking about the possibility of* you moving in." But he didn't hear the first part of my sentence ...
Rachmiel:	I thought she was formally asking me to move in.

Shefa:	His face got real serious.
Rachmiel:	Yeah, I got real quiet because that's an important decision. I've been married twice myself. And I said "I need to take it inside and really think about it and I'll give you my answer."
	It took me about a week. I really had to be sure. Throughout all the wrangling with myself, there was a part that was so clear: I was supposed to be with Shefa. So I came back to her and I said "Yes."
	It was only after I had moved in and some friends were here for *Pesach* and she told the story that I realized that I'd missed her saying, "let's talk about the possibility."
Shefa:	We thought maybe there was an angel distracting him during the first part of the sentence.
Rachmiel:	So, I moved in on April 1st anyway. We did a commitment ceremony with two friends of ours.
	So we're living together a few months and I really didn't even know what Shefa did because I had never seen her do anything.
	And it wasn't until August of 2000 when I went to *Elat Chaim* (Jewish Renewal retreat camp) for the first time that I knew that I wanted to live together with Shefa for the rest of my life.
	There were a lot of really cool Jewish Renewal people there drumming and dancing and chanting. And I thought, "Oh, this is my tribe." But it was during that week when something in my heart lifted. I was in our little room standing and looking out the windows, out towards the pool and the beautiful land right in front of me, and there was a Presence in my heart that said, "You."
	And I knew I wanted to marry her, not just spend the rest of my life with this woman, but marry her.

	I wanted to move into a spiritual joining, a really sacred union.
	I'd never actually had a sacred... My two marriages were with the justice of the peace. I never had a ceremony. A ceremony would be like taking me to the next level of commitment of living with someone and being partnered with someone, to a level I hadn't been before, ever.
Shefa:	Meanwhile there were all these people there who loved me and needed to vet him to make sure that he wasn't going to break my heart.
Rachmiel:	But I accepted that with appreciation, thinking, "Well, they must really care about Shefa a lot. I totally understand this." So, I was completely open to it. I passed the screening obviously.
Marilyn:	How would they check you out?
Rachmiel:	That same very first week at *Elat Chaim*, three other couples took us out to dinner. And after dinner they led a grilling of me.
Shefa:	They're kind of family for me.
Rachmiel:	Yeah. So, it was very formal, very like, "Okay. What are your intentions? Who are you? What's going on?"
Marilyn:	They were like the collective father interviewing the prospective bridegroom.
Rachmiel:	Exactly. When Phyllis was talking to me and challenging me and asking me questions, I had that meta-awareness that they must love Shefa so much. And even though this was a low pass, I knew I was going to pass through unscathed, because I was the right one.
Philip:	Shefa, did you know that they were vetting him?
Shefa:	Oh yeah. Yeah.
Philip:	Did they clear that with you?

Shefa:	I don't think that they had to clear it. They're my family. We were all protective of each other that way. It was expected.
Marilyn:	**How has being in this relationship transformed you?**
Shefa:	In the beginning of our relationship we shared an important way of playing. Our drumming and chanting was a way for us to enter into sacred space together.

There was something about Rachmiel's drumming that would open up melodies for me.

I could hear inside the rhythm of his drumming the melody that wanted to come through. So, there was this wonderful synergy, a mystical bonding. Rachmiel hasn't been able to drum for many years, but I think that connection between us still stayed.

I'm very sensitive to energy. I know when energy is built up inside me and needs to be released. But I never knew how to do that exactly. Rachmiel taught me how to do that.

When one of us gets tense, we say to the other person, "I think I need a session." That's a sign that the other person needs to listen in a very different way. When you're listening to someone having a session, you're not trying to fix anything and you suspend all judgment.

You just create a sacred space for that person to release whatever it is; they can cry, or shake or just rant, but it's not anything that you engage with. And at the end of the session, there's a kind of clarity.

I feel like it is such an incredible saving grace in our relationship. Before that, my tendency might be to pick a fight with somebody because I would be upset about something or irritable.

I can say, "I think I need a session," and Rachmiel knows how to sit with me. Sometimes I can just look at him and I say, "Do you need a session?"

And I know that if I don't do that, he'll start getting crabby and irritable or something, and we'll end up unhappy. But if we just take 10 minutes to have the session, then the love can flow and we can be clear again.

I think that our relationship really depends on each of us being self-aware of what our own energy state is.

Once when Rachmiel and I were having some kind of argument... It was a kind of argument where in the middle of it, you don't even know what you're arguing about. We called timeout and each of us went to our meditation room and I started to do this chant of mine that's all about finding the depths inside you.

(At this point she sang this lovely chant for us.)

> *Ku mah Adonai, Hosheani Elohai*
> *Ku mah Adonai, Hosheani Elohai*

So, what that means is

> *Rise up, the God place inside me.*
> *Rise up, and save me.*

Like, save me from my *Mishegas* (Craziness). Save me from the surface of irritability. In relationships, it's usually what's on the surface that gets tangled up,

But if I can go to the deeper place inside me, then I find this spaciousness and clarity and love and calm, but I don't always have access to it.

And so, I think a lot of the practices that we do are how we access what's our deepest intention, what's the deepest place inside us. So after doing that practice, then we could come back together.

Rachmiel:	So I was probably downstairs tapping while she's upstairs chanting and then...
Marilyn:	I love it. He's downstairs tapping while you're upstairs chanting. Can you tell us more about the practices you mentioned?
Shefa:	We're always looking for lots of tools that change your energy state and bring you back to wholeness.

That's also what we teach at our leadership training. Because if you're in leadership, and if you don't have that self-awareness of your own state, then you'll be coming from a place of being triggered; and that's not your highest wisdom or your greatest love.

And Rachmiel is very dedicated to his spiritual practice and it helps me to stay disciplined in my practice. He's doing his practice, so it's hard for me to slack off.

David Schnarch teaches that there are these Points of Differentiation where you have to do your work.

For example: How can you be yourself when you're with someone who's different than you? How can you be close to someone else and not feel like you're going to get lost in some way? How can you hold on to the way you're different and learn how to not be critical of the other person who's different than you?

How can you really accept and appreciate those differences. That's the first point.

And then there's learning how to self-sooth. If I can't regulate my own anxiety, then I'm going to try to manipulate my partner to help me to try to get me to feel better. That's the second point.

So, I think what helps in our relationship is we're always looking how to grow in those areas.

Yesterday, I got very flustered because my phone wasn't working, the Internet wasn't working and all the technology in our house was falling apart. And I really could feel that I needed to do something that would help me sooth myself or else I would be trying to get Rachmiel to make me feel better. And it just doesn't work that way.

For me, my relationship with God needs to be the primary relationship. Then the overflow comes to Rachmiel. Then I'm not looking to him to do what only God can do for me.

So what happened that time was that Rachmiel, instead of trying to fix it, which would have been the old pattern, just acknowledged my frustration and said, "Yeah, I know it's hard."

Rachmiel: And she fixed it herself.

Shefa: Another of the points of differentiation is tolerating discomfort for growth. I reminded myself, "Oh, yeah, this is uncomfortable. This is going to pass."

Dr. David Schnarch's "Passionate Marriage" approach to couples has really informed us a lot in the everyday nitty-gritty. When you get into the emotional gridlock, he gets excited and says, "Great, you're about to have an evolutionary breakthrough." I mean, it is breakup or breakthrough. But he says, "There's nothing wrong with you when you're in that place." You are both trying to evolve, to go to a new creation.

I see my main practice as taking every moment of my life and feeling myself addressed by God, the Beloved, and also addressing God. Then I can be with Rachmiel from the overflow of that relationship. Instead of coming to him with my neediness, I'm coming to him with the fullness of this love that I have for God's Reality. So Rachmiel then gets the benefit of me being in love with Life.

	And so it's a different expectation of the relationship, because we get into tangles when I'm expecting him to be what I want him to be. And he's clearly not going to do that. This way I could be surprised and delighted by who he is.
Rachmiel:	Yes, I have that place, too, when I'm connected up to the Source. "Then streams come forth from Eden toward the Garden." When I'm experiencing that, then my relationship with Shefa goes better. And when I'm not there, then it's really my own work to reconnect.
	Although I can ask Shefa for help, to be an ally, if I expect her to make me feel better, or say the right thing, or do the right thing, all those crazy things... I don't want to do that.
Shefa:	There was a moment early in our relationship when Rachmiel said to me, "I'm so glad that you love God more than you love me." He really got it. He really got it that that was what I had to give.
Philip:	**Do you see your relationship as a kind of spiritual practice?**
Shefa:	Sometimes I think of our relationship not as our spiritual practice, but more as the measure of it. I can tell how strong my practice is by what comes up in our relationship. So, if I'm not grounded, not connected inside myself, then the relationship is not going to go smoothly.
	I think that in the work I do of being a spiritual teacher, I'm always very aware of what's in my heart. And if I leave something undone or unresolved, it actually takes the energy away from my presence as a leader. So it becomes this daily practice, what I called "clearing away the ashes on the altar of my heart so that the fires of my heart can really burn clear."
Rachmiel:	Something I've been working on is projection and what that really means. I mean, I knew the concept. I have my Masters in Counseling and all that.

I read about projecting on other people and I read Carl Jung's statement that the best thing we can do for someone is to remove our projections from them. But I swear, knowing all of that, I didn't realize how much I was still projecting onto Shefa.

A small example is that sometimes, I would experience Shefa as being abrupt, or just dismissing me. And I would get so upset and I would think in my mind that that's not how I treat her. I don't do that. And then, at some point, as conscious and aware of myself as I was, I realized that I did do that, too. It was a projection. I was being abrupt and dismissive to her. And then I realized, maybe I'm projecting a whole lot of stuff onto her that I'm totally unconscious of.

That's Schnarch's Passionate Marriage work and in that work, those kinds of difficulties are exciting because they mean we're about to evolve.

Shefa: One of the great things in our relationship is Rachmiel's vow to me that he would only make new mistakes.

Rachmiel: Sometimes quite a few of them.

Philip: Would you be willing to share a story about one of those about-to-evolve, break-through moments?

Shefa: So after Rachmiel's surgery, his daughter wanted to come and visit. And I knew this was not a good time for her to come because she wasn't really coming to help. She was coming because she wanted a vacation.

But as the stepmother, it's hard for me to say "no." I really wanted Rachmiel to say "no," but he was just letting things go, saying, "It's going to be okay."

Afterwards he understood and he was able to say, "I made a mistake here.

I should have been the one to say "no, this isn't the right time." I didn't have to make a big fight about that because he was owning that for himself.

And so when we really stop and take those moments, I think they are very holy moments. Because if one of us makes a mistake and can say, "This is something I'm never going to do again," they are bringing a lot of attention and love to that moment.

We are really keeping to that vow that we are only going to make new mistakes.

Rachmiel: That was such an important growing for us because at first, when we started talking about it, I felt defensive.

Of course I wanted to protect my daughter. But I didn't get lost in that emotion. I really wanted to work this out with Shefa.

At first, I thought it was just about me wanting Shefa to be the one to say, "No, I don't want her to come."

But that didn't feel right. Then, I had this "ah-hah" moment and I understood what it might be like for Shefa as a step-parent to have to be the one to say "no". That's a terrible position to be in.

If we had just stopped at each of us saying to the other, "No, you need be more assertive," I wouldn't have gotten it and I would have done it again. But I really, really got it and I said, "I don't want to put you in that position. I will step up and do whatever."

That was wonderful. And then it was clear. We worked it through. It's just gone.

Marilyn: **Are there aspects of yourselves that your partner values that you didn't value so much when you were younger, parts of yourself that you're learning to appreciate?**

Shefa: Well, for me it's the way I love to feed other people and take care of things. I didn't have children but the Great Mother energy pours through me. I don't think I was very aware of it, or appreciated that in myself. But when I met Rachmiel, I felt like he saw that very soft and vulnerable mothering part of me.

Rachmiel: I just remember once Shefa had come home from a trip, and then, the next day, she was in the kitchen, cooking up a big meal. I was laughing and saying to my daughter, "She just travels the world and comes home and gets in the kitchen to cook to get grounded."

For my part, the quality I'm thinking of is my sensitivity. I was born in 1950. Growing up in that time as a young boy my whole sensitive, intuitive side was not encouraged. In my relationship with Shefa, she encourages that part. We do some healing work together and it lets that part of me flower.

And the same is true about my music. That's the one thing I've done throughout my life. I started playing guitar and then moved into drumming. I can remember my parents saying, "Well, yeah, but how are you going to make a living at it? The gift is really nice, but you got to get a real job." And recently, while we were doing an evening chanting and I was using my musical talents, I had a flashback to my early growing up. And I felt, as a matter of fact, I am using my musical talent, and receiving money for it, and in such a holy and sacred way, more than I could have ever imagined. I felt so proud.

Philip: You've really reclaimed a lot, your music and your sensitivity, and you name it as being holy and sacred. How then do you connect all that with your Judaism and how does that connect to your marriage to Shefa?

Rachmiel: In the spring of 2000 I met Reb Zalman Schachter-Shalomi for the first time. He's the grandfather of Jewish Renewal, and he said to me, "You'd be welcome to come into Judaism. Your earth-based spirituality and Judaism just go hand-in-hand. It's a great fit." He said, "Try all of the treasures in Judaism and if you get juice from it, take it as yours. And if you don't, just put it aside. You don't need to do it."

With that kind of freedom, oh my God! I live a Jewish life cycle through the year, but it's totally because I get juice from it.

Philip **Now Shefa, what is the connection between your relationship with Rachmiel and your Judaism?**

Shefa: For me, it's very tied up, me and Judaism. Rachmiel encountered us both at the same time. I sort of mediate his relationship with Judaism. And I'm very protective, so I only let him know all those cool things.

Also I benefit because I have my eyes opened to certain things through Rachmiel.

Rachmiel: Because I didn't have any baggage about Judaism.

Shefa: So, I could re-experience things through him and see what an incredible treasure was there. As he was discovering it, I got to rediscover it.

My book, *Torah Journeys,* is a book about that.

It's asking "What's the blessing? What is the spiritual challenge? And what's the practice that I can do in order to enter into Torah?" It's a way of experiencing Torah through our own experience. It's reading the text as if it's not about somebody else, but it's about me and it's about this very moment.

So, he was learning Torah through me. And we interacted at this level of Torah together. It was a very important part of writing. I would write a chapter and give it to him and he would send it back to me with all the red pen marks on it.

	Torah has become an important part of our relationship in that way. Every week we read aloud a chapter from *Torah Journeys* and do the practices together.
Rachmiel:	Yeah, it all just happened so naturally. I didn't feel anything forced. And I did the conversion inclusion ceremony at the Jewish Renewal retreat camp in August of '01 before we got married and it was a wonderful spiritual experience.
Shefa:	So, we get to co-create what Judaism is for us in our home. We're really creating that for ourselves.
Marilyn:	**So *Torah Journeys* came out of your relationship with each other. And at the same time you met Rachmiel, you were starting to study *Song of Songs* and eventually there was a book on that. What's the interaction between that book and your relationship?**
Shefa:	I started to go to a deeper level of what I was learning from the Song of Songs in terms of how to live each moment of my life in relationship to the Beloved and how the Beloved appears.
Rachmiel:	The basis of it all for me is to live *Shir Ha'Sharim,* The Song of Songs. How do we live that as a true, genuine model?

One time, years ago, when I found myself raising my voice at Shefa and we were arguing, I actually had the presence of mind to stop and say, "Wait a minute, look at the couple in the Song of Songs, they don't talk to each other like this." And it completely diffused whatever we were arguing about and we worked it out.

We keep going back to the foundation of *Shir Ha'Sharim.* How do we be with each other and with God and help our relationship?

That's what we wrote in our *Ketubah* (marriage contract).

	We wrote "Let the Great Love come through me to you."
Shefa:	In Judaism there are all these rules about *Lashon Horah* (evil tongue), about what you shouldn't say. What I learned from the Song of Songs is that the lovers are always saying, "Oh, how beautiful you are. You're perfect." There's this incredible flow of generosity that we've taken on as a lifestyle. Every Wednesday morning we wake up and we say "Happy Trash Day!" Here's another reason to celebrate, to love each other. That daily paying attention to appreciating one another, it's not a way I've lived before.
Rachmiel:	I remember consciously saying after another relationship ended, "I just want somebody who would just hang in with me and do the work when it gets really tough." And we do that. I've never had that before. In any other relationship, if things got too bad, they ended.
	Before my first surgery when I was really just out of my mind with pain and I didn't have enough attention to keep doing the work, I just wanted a break. I couldn't keep going and things were tense. And that was totally exacerbated by this intense, constant chronic headache that I finally had two surgeries for. In the back of my mind, I thought, "Maybe I'll go stay with my folks for a few weeks, just to release the pressure." I just hung in. Even though you make a commitment there's some times where you don't want to do it. Yeah. You just want a break.
Shefa:	I was just remembering this moment. You were sitting right there and in a bad mood. This is one of the first times. I think it was a breakthrough in our relationship. You were very grumpy.
Rachmiel:	Grumpy?

Shefa:	But I was in a very spacious place in my own heart. I said, "It's okay that you're in a bad mood. You're allowed to have that." And I remember him looking at me like, "Oh." He felt like I wasn't going to resist where he was emotionally at that moment. I was making space for it and saying, "My love is big enough to hold your bad mood and I'm not going to be reactive to it." And I think it shifted everything in that moment. It was one of those realizations that there could be room for all of us. I think one of the main principles of our relationship is to tune in to what is the other's deepest intention. So if he's in a lot of pain or something like that and it seems that he doesn't have good intentions, what I need to do is tune in to his deepest intention, which is to love me. I think that's what we call in Judaism, *Kaf Sechut,* the scale plan of merit, giving them the benefit of the doubt.
Philip:	**So you've been challenged and you rise to it with love.**
Shefa:	I think in our relationship now, Rachmiel's physical situation has been one of the main challenges. When he's feeling well, he gives me such good attention, which I love. But when he's in pain, he doesn't have it to give, so, I have to not try to get it.
Rachmiel:	No matter what, pain or not, I want to really have kindness in my voice. I do not want to let myself get triggered. I want to avoid ever having a certain tone in my voice towards my beloved. As in the Song of Songs, that's how I want to live, with that much impeccability. So I want to be my most impeccable self as I turn 60 and in this next part of my life. But the Practice in the relationship, this is the hardest. If I can do it here, I can do it anywhere.

For more information about Rabbi Shefa's books, CD's, classes, personal appearances, and workshops
http://rabbishefagold.com/

Rabbi Shefa and Rachmiel
The Blue Thread in Their Love Story

"Turn and return ... that I may gaze upon you."
From In the Fever of Love. An Illumination of the Song of Songs
by Shefa Gold

If you were to plant two young trees in a yard, as those trees grew, their roots and trunks would intertwine. However, if you were to plant two full grown trees in a yard, you'd have to put them far enough apart to allow for their separate root systems. They could still touch each other but only through the fullness of their branches.

Shefa and Rachmiel are two mature people. They have their own separate spiritual roots which are very explicitly not part of their relationship. They go there for nourishment and then return to the relationship renewed.

We can see this in their Genesis stories. Both Shefa and Rachmiel remember the moment that they each knew. They were each alone. Each accessed an inner resource. Shefa's moment came when she was getting a massage and she received a vision, a visit from Eliahu. Rachmiel's moment came when he was alone in his room and he felt a Presence in his heart and he heard a voice saying "You."

These private experiences are still crucial. Rachmiel talks about going to "Source." Shefa talks about the time she spends in her relationship with God.

Shefa: *My relationship with God needs to be my primary relationship. Then the overflow comes to Rachmiel. Then I'm not looking to him to do what only God can do for me.*

Rachmiel: *Yes, I have that place, too, when I'm connected up to the Source. ... Although I can ask Shefa for help, to be an ally, if I expect her to make me feel better, or say the right thing, or do the right thing, all those crazy things... I don't want to do that.*

This is the blue thread for us, the reminder that there is a Source, a resource, independent of the relationship which one can visit and revisit and each time return to the relationship renewed. Turn and Return.

Many couples understand this as they mature. They learn over time to not try to be everything to each other, each partner has to be aware of, and responsible for his or her own center of gravity.

> Shefa: *Sometimes I think of our relationship not as our spiritual practice, but more as the measure of it. I can tell how strong my spiritual practice is by what comes up in our relationship. So, if I'm not grounded, not connected inside myself, then the relationship is not going to go smoothly.*

There are limits to what we can expect of our partner in a marriage. We must each be responsible for how we manage our emotions, our energy, our irritability, our resentments, our secret desires, our longings, our disappointments, our attractions, our *Mishagas* (craziness) as Shefa calls it, using very technical Rabbinic language.

Shefa and Rachmiel are both very clear that they are committed to their own spiritual path. They want the other person to be similarly committed. In this framework their partner is not the center of their universe. Rachmiel says he is glad Shefa *"loves God more than me."* In turn, Shefa is delighted that Rachmiel fell in love with Shabbas before he fell in love with her.

Now here is the fine line. Shefa says that she goes to God and opens up again and "Rachmiel gets the overflow." "Overflow" is not the same as "leftovers." When Shefa says "overflow," she means "abundance." (And by the way, Shefa's chosen name is Hebrew for "Abundance.") Shefa's and Rachmiel's individual spiritual practices are rich. They want to bring as much to their relationship.

> Rachmiel: *How do we be with each other and with God and help our relationship?*

Shefa: What I learned from the Song of Songs is that the lovers are always saying, "Oh, how beautiful you are. You're perfect." There's this incredible flow of generosity that we've taken on as a lifestyle.

This is how we understand "Turn and Return," which is what the lovers do in the Song of Songs. You go to your sanctuary, you fill yourself up with love and then return to your Lover. The flow starts with God. The overflow goes to each other. And then it gets even bigger. The overflow of that love (remember the kissing meditation) goes out and blesses the world.

Chapter Six

Looking for Lilith

Rabbi Ohad and Dawn Cherie Ezrahi

It took me years to learn how to walk my talk, to be present and loving in the face of the feminine storm, the emotional storm, and not to run away. ...
I wrote about Lilith, but still, this is the difference between theory and practice. – Ohad

He wrote about Lilith but he wasn't ready to deal with her. – Dawn

Legend has it that Lilith was Adam's first wife and she refused to "lie under Adam" so she had to leave the Garden. Then God said to Adam, "It's not good for you to be alone" and He created Eve using a piece of Adam as the basic material, the theory being that she would be more subservient, a "good girl," although, as you know, it didn't turn out that way.

But what happened to Lilith, the independent woman? Oh, people had bad things to say about her. They said she's a demon who eats babies. Her spirit lives on in prostitutes. She haunts men's dreams, takes their nocturnal semen and gives birth to more demons. Good people should fear her. Ohad felt called to write a scholarly text about Lilith to challenge those beliefs. He argued that the Lilith story was about a brilliant, creative, free spirited woman who was so powerful that Adam simply couldn't face her. A man should appreciate such a woman, instead of condemning her. He should partner with her. That's what Ohad wrote.

Then he met Dawn.

Marilyn: **When did you first realize Ohad was going to be a significant person in your life?**

Dawn: When I met Ohad I was at Elat Chayyim, Center for Jewish Renewal in a two-year training course for prayer leadership. I was camping out by the lake and I was going to the shower. I remember seeing him, his energy. He wasn't my teacher; He was teaching another course. It clicked in my mind that this is the kind of man that I could see myself being with. I didn't go "Oh, this is The Man, this is it, this is my *beshert*," but something in my heart just said, "This feels right."

But, I didn't know. Maybe there were a lot of these kinds of men wandering around. This was my first week there. But then, it proved to be that there is really only one Ohad.

Ohad: So I was just arriving, basically, and it was my first time teaching in Elat Chayyim, and I got the Rabbi's cabin. I was looking out from the window and here I see a beautiful woman walking towards the swimming pool and the hot tub, walking across the grass. She was wearing turquoise.

Dawn: Like a sarong or something.

Ohad: Yeah, like clothes. It magnetized me immediately. I wanted to see her. I was actually hoping that she was going to go into the hot tub and take off her clothes. So I get my guitar and go sit out on the balcony, looking out and playing guitar as if, you know, I'm not doing it for her.

Dawn: But I pretended not to see him.

Ohad: She was ignoring me basically. That was our first seeing each other.

Dawn: I had a friend who was there, Menacheim, and he was engaged to Wendy, who was Ohad's friend, and that night I joined the two of them in a conversation in the dining hall.

Ohad: Yeah. I just went to have a cup of tea in the dining hall and there's Menacheim and Wendy sitting, and Dawn was sitting with them. So I had a great excuse. I came and sat with them at the table and we started to speak.

Dawn: But I was playing it cool, you know. I was in a training course. I had a week there. I didn't want to get someone so fast.

Ohad: She said she was there studying davening, prayer. And of course I teased her with, like, "Do you know that in the Hassidic tradition, prayer is considered lovemaking with the Shechina *(The Feminine manifestation of God)*?" And she was blooming, shining from ear to ear. My kind of girl. Then we went outside and there was an awkward moment. I didn't ask anything and she didn't. And so we say, "Goodnight. Goodnight."

Dawn: "Goodnight. Goodnight." You know, it is the second night or something. So play it cool.

Ohad: And then – And then I couldn't sleep all night.

Dawn: He sleeps great. Now, I know this, he sleeps like a log.

Ohad: I usually sleep very good, but that night, something was ... she was in my heart so strong. And it wasn't just, you know, sexual fantasy or something. It was, like, really something was moving me. So I really had a hard time falling asleep.

Dawn: So then in the morning when we saw each other...

Ohad: In the breakfast.

Dawn: In the breakfast. And I said, "So how'd you sleep?" checking to see how it was for him. And he said, "Not very well."

Ohad: And then I said, "And you?" And she said, "As well." And I said, "For the same reasons?" And she said, "Yeah."

Dawn: So then it was clear. There was a little energy, a little juice. Because you never know.

Ohad: In the morning I went to listen to the class that she was taking. And then lunch came and I asked her to go to swim in the river. And she said yes.

So we started to walk to the river and on the way I told her, "Look, I'm very attracted to you but... and... you need to know that I'm not a monogamous person." I'm putting all my eggs in one basket. Not only am I telling her that I'm attracted to her, I'm also telling her in the same sentence that I'm not monogamous. But I wanted to be very honest with her.

Dawn: Which was good for me. That was the lifestyle choice that I had wanted.

Ohad: Her response was so sweet. It was like, "Yeah, me too!" So that was basically our first intimate talk.

Dawn: Right. And then we went down to the lake and there was a nice energy but it wasn't... I'm sort of naïve in some ways. I really am. Like, unless someone, boom, hits me over the head, or kisses me, I'm "Oh, okay, you really... you really like me now? Oh. Okay.

So we had our first kiss under the waterfall. And I remember when he started to kiss, it was like "Oh my! Butterflies!" My stomach flip-flopped.

	And then I was like, "Oh-oh, this is going to be a ride. My life isn't going to be the same. I can tell." And it hasn't been.
Ohad:	Yep. The rest is history.
Dawn:	The rest is history.
Marilyn:	So then what happened after that? You definitely got us locked into the story.
Dawn:	So he came to New York after and visited me but I was very entrenched in my life. We talked often and started emailing. He found ways to come several times in that year.

The first visit was in December. It was cold and snowy and he came to BJ's, (B'nai Jeshurun Synagogue) where I belonged. He was a guest teacher and he said, "Come on, you're teaching with me." I'm like "What? I don't know. I don't want to teach." Because it was my congregation I was very happy just being, just sitting and praying. |
| Ohad: | I saw the teacher in her. I was like, "What? You're not teaching? That's unbelievable. You have to teach. Come teach with me."

That was December. At that time I was heading a Jewish Ashram, a residential intentional community, really radical and a lot of fun. We were exploring, living very, very simply in what we call "caravans," little trailers, in the middle of nothing in the desert overlooking the Dead Sea. |
| Dawn: | Totally different from New York City; really beautiful, but rugged. |
| Ohad: | Somehow, with God's help, I managed to be invited to teach in New York in December and then in March. I had put New York as a high priority. |

	I was just ending my marriage of 16 years. We separated in a very good way. We did a very nice ceremony in the community and...
Dawn:	And I remember when he called me and he said he got divorced. And it was like "Ooooh, this is real." Like before then, I didn't know. Like when we had met they were already separated, but you know how life is. Couples make reconciliation. So I remember talking to Ohad and I felt like, "Wow! This is serious."
	Something shifted for me. I started to make the moves. I planned my first trip to Israel. I always planned to go to Israel but somehow, before, it never manifested.
Ohad:	So I took her from New York City to the Dead Sea in August.
Dawn:	So hot. I couldn't believe it. I mean, I'm from Buffalo, New York, what do I know of this heat? It was like an oven. And then I came and had the best falafel in the country. And then, meeting the community ...
Ohad:	It was an Ashram, a very intimate community.
Dawn:	The ex-wife was living next door with this little paper-thin door between us, so, I heard her, she heard us, and the three kids were going back and forth. She was very lovely. She was the first one, really, that came and welcomed me in a good way.
Ohad:	Yes. She took care that Dawn would feel well and welcomed. She actually gave us a double bed and said "Welcome to your new life."
	And then everybody was coming to see this American girl that took my heart. Who is she? Some were happy. Some were a little jealous, maybe.

Dawn: Yeah. Yeah. It was intense. I remember them, one after another coming in and saying, "Hello, I'm so-and-so. Welcome." It was surreal, with the heat and mosquito netting, so different from anything I had known. There were camels.

This was not New York City.

Philip: **Were you ready for a change of that magnitude?**

Dawn: It was a time when I was looking for change in my life. When I met Ohad, it definitely made sense for my life story. If I had met a guy from Zimbabwe or something, I might not have considered it as much.

I was thinking that I wanted to move out of New York, perhaps Woodstock, perhaps Colorado. Well, Israel was a little more of a radical shift.

But it was not only the place. I had dated so many men in New York and I hate to say it, so many neurotic, Jewish men. I was tired, and this was so different. Ohad just kept coming up as the most authentic, the most sensitive, real person. And I tested him like crazy. He had some quality that made him hard to resist, and hard to give up. I tried to give him up but I couldn't. We had a sharing of common values, of rituals, of the way of looking at life as a kind of adventure. And the one thing I knew is that I would never be bored with Ohad.

Ohad: Yeah. For me there was something in the energy of Dawn that was really playing directly into my heart. Already I had been studying how the sages of the Talmud described how, in the Temple of Solomon, there were two golden figures, Cherubim, and they were making love.

During the rites of pilgrimage, the priests would open the curtains and show the Cherubim to the crowds and say, "See, the love of God to you is like the love of a male and a female."

Making love was the only symbol for the connection with the divine. It was the highest expression of spirituality. This was the ancient Hebraic Path.

Meeting Dawn played directly into my heart. We were those two Cherubs.

Rabbinical Judaism went far away from that ancient Hebraic Path. Years before, when I was still an Ultra-Orthodox Jew and was teaching in Yeshiva in Jerusalem,

I started to see that the way Judaism relates to the body and to sex is really different from the ancient way, and it was an unspoken issue. I devoted myself to this research and published a book about the Two Cherubs, in which I pointed out the erotic aspect of the temple in Jerusalem. I was literally amazed by the textual findings I found all over, biblical stuff, Kabbalistic stuff, Talmudic support.

Some Orthodox Rabbis said that, though it is all true, I shouldn't publish the book. These kinds of things should not be out there. I thought the opposite. This was in 1997, and it marks the beginning of my stepping out of the Orthodox world.

So for years before we met I was already looking for the way to live Eros as a sacred thing. I already understood that we should embody the Cherubs in our human love. But how? I was waiting for a partner I could go deep with and explore it with. And then, along came Dawn as a divine gift.

Marilyn: **You had this vision of combining the spiritual and the erotic. This seems to have captured your imagination but at that time you were living a very different reality, a very traditional life, right?**

Ohad: When I met Dawn I was already non-Orthodox. I was transitioning slowly, over the years, from ultra Orthodoxy to a more modern unorthodoxy. And then I left it altogether in 2000.

Dawn: Yeah, like you moved from the black *payos* (*side locks*) and the black hat to the rainbow yarmulke; still the *payos*, but more kind of hippy.

Marilyn: So did your relationship with your wife back then start to change because of that?

Ohad: No, not really. My wife came with me a long way. We were girlfriend and boyfriend in a secular, environmental high school and, afterwards, we both together went into the religious world. Neither of us grew up religious and we both made the journey from the secular world to the ultra-Orthodox and out of it to establish the Ashram together in the Judean desert.

But she really wanted a family, a regular family, and I wanted to explore more around Eros in a less monogamous way and that was not for her. Some of the exploration we did together. We were good friends for many, many years, but eventually I was left to do it alone. And I wondered when I would be able to really change my life and be able to walk my talk.

I definitely had made the first mental steps through my Kabalistic research. Then I said, I said, "Okay, now I need to live this." And then God brought me the manifestation. Dawn came to my life. It just all made sense. It was like "Okay, let's go."

Marilyn: **On your part, Dawn, was there a parallel process?**

Dawn: Well while he was living his ultra-Orthodox life in Israel, I was in Paris doing high-fashion modeling. So, at that point, we were very worlds apart. I made my own journey, going to the College of the Atlantics to study Human Ecology, living on an organic farm off the grid in Maine, and then making my way back to New York City.

I was always a spiritual seeker even when I was in high school. I remember one time, putting all my pillows in a closet and making a little isolation tank and thinking "Okay, there's got to be something in this suburban lifestyle that's better than this."

One day I realized that everything I was doing in New York was a search for spirit, for more peace. I was head of a ritual theater company. I was studying a lot with women, women's mystery schools, and priestessing. And always, while making love and having boy-friends; it always made sense to me to have a life of spirit, a life where sexuality was more sacred.

And just before I met Ohad I had discovered the work of David Deida. He has a book called, *Finding God Through Sex*. He's one of the best teachers on sacred sexuality.

Ohad: And Sacred Relationships.

Dawn: So when I brought the work of David Deida to Ohad, he said "This is *Hassidut (the teaching of Hassidic mysticism)*, exactly what I've been studying, just in a different vocabulary. I have to meet this guy!" So we met David and took many intensives with him.

	But even before we studied with David, there was always a quality of sacredness in our lovemaking, of really setting a prayer, an intention to make *Love*. Sometimes we felt like, "How can I contain all this pleasure? It feels selfish almost." And, so through our lovemaking, we started sending it out as a prayer to the people in our lives. It became so potent that it became one of our ways of praying.

Philip: Has anything ever happened that made you think, "Oh, okay, this really works, it's not just a pretty idea"?

Ohad: Yeah, for me things just clicked during our sessions of lovemaking, like, "Wow, now I understand."

Kabalistic things that would later take me a half a year to teach, I would just get in one lovemaking. It would just fall into place. Sometimes I would write poetry. I would get music or lyrics for a song during a session of lovemaking and as soon as we were through I would go and write it down immediately. I remember Dawn would say, "Muse me."

Dawn: It's transpersonal love, where you are not denying what you see through the person. You go in through them, beyond them.

You use them as a temple, a divine conduit for communicating, for prayer, for contact with the divine.

When I married Ohad, it was not only because we really loved each other as people. We are each other's conduit to Love. I am able to love God through his body and he through mine.

We see our relationship as a spiritual container. Sometimes we do rituals and sometimes we light candles but it's not about that.

	It's more about what's happening here, between us. This can be enough for a temple. This is enough.
Philip:	That's so beautiful. Something gets revealed beyond your immediate love-making. For you, Dawn, it's a prayer you send out to those you care about.
Marilyn:	And for you, Ohad, it's an insight into the deeper meaning of some of the Kabbalistic teachings.
Philip:	**Those are deep waters. Are there challenges too?**
Ohad:	Challenges? Many. Dawn is really a free-spirited feminine. Big emotions. And I come from being a scholar.
Dawn:	I'm a Scorpio, he's a Libra.
Ohad:	Yeah. I'm a Libra so there's a part of me that likes harmony.
Dawn:	And I like drama.
Ohad:	And she likes drama.
Dawn:	I'm a woman; he's a man.
Ohad:	It took me years to learn how to walk my talk, to be present and loving in the face of the feminine storm, the emotional storm, and not to run away or crumble.
Dawn:	I remember, in the beginning of our relationship, getting so irritated at him because he wouldn't get me, or he would apologize in such an abominable way. He would say, "Oh, I'm sorry" and then immediately go to justify it. I was like "Agh!" It was so frustrating.

Ohad: You need to understand – I learned English while being with Dawn.

Dawn: He really didn't know the language and I spoke almost no Hebrew.

Ohad: Many times, just because of lack of skills in the language, I just expressed myself very poorly and she didn't get what I meant. She took what I said ...

Dawn: Literally.

Ohad: Literally and it was really horrible.

So, okay, a story: Since we had a long – how do you call it? – cross-ocean relationship, sometimes I said something over the phone that was very upsetting to her. The truth is she didn't understand and I didn't know what I said wrong.

Even so, when she would get upset, my practice was not to say, "Okay, go fuck yourself and see me when you're done," but to call her again and to be present, even if she hung up on me. I would call back and say "I'm with you, I love you. Let's see what's there."

I even wrote a song paraphrasing Rumi's poem. I composed it for her as a gift of love. The lyrics are, "Beyond the words there's a field, I will see you there. Will I see you there, see you there?" Basically, I was saying, "Let's meet beyond the words because my language is getting between us." We recorded it some years ago. [It is on their CD, "Something out of Chaos."] So that's a story of offering my heart in a song as a healing.

Another time Dawn was in this one-woman show in New York and I said something to her and it was as if I were criticizing her more than I meant to. She got really hurt and upset. It created a big drama and a big emotion.

Big emotion. I felt attacked. It was a test for me. How do I deal with it? Do I go away? It was really too much, beyond my comfort zone, a lot beyond my comfort zone.

So I went out and I walked around the block and I prayed to God like, "Please show me. How do I deal with this power of the Feminine? How do I meet her in love – not escaping, not freaking out, not checking out?" And I came back to the apartment with this decision -- I'm stepping in, I'm not stepping out. The great thing about Dawn is that she did not hang on to her anger. She immediately responded to my presence with her open heart.

Anger was my big fear. I wanted harmony and quiet and here I am with this theater actress – Life is theater and drama – a big feminine, expressive woman. So there are many moments like that of me learning how to deal with ...

Dawn: He wrote about Lilith but he wasn't ready to deal with her.

Ohad: Yeah I was writing about Lilith before I met Dawn so I was interacting with this energy, but still, this is the difference between theory and practice.

Philip: So you fear this feminine power and also have a fascination with it. What would be the difference in the way you deal with that power now and the way you did it when you were younger?

Ohad: Oh there is a big difference. My regular response or reaction would be to shut down, to go to my corner, to go to study something, to go to pray, to go to meditate. "She's attacking me." "I'm right, of course." And, "She's going crazy so it's not my job, she needs to calm down."

Dawn: Yuck!

Ohad: And now instead of doing that and staying in my "I'm right" cave, I step out of the cave and meet her with love. Instead of taking refuge from the storm, I'm charging the storm with an open heart. That feels like danger. It feels really dangerous. I guess with many men the big fear is feminine emotions, women and emotions, like war is less frightening.

Marilyn: **How about on your side? What are the challenges for you?**

Dawn: I came from a very emotionally aware place, working a lot with the body and emotions and being able to verbalize problems. I came through the self-help world. Ohad was coming from the spirit world which was clearly different. We had different languages.

I knew that this man had the raw material. He had the stuff that was really important.

But when I met him 10 years ago, he wasn't skilled in being able to verbalize what was happening. I felt that there was some training that needed to happen.

I remember there was one time. This was really pivotal. We were going to a David Deida workshop in New York and we were late leaving the house.

I expected Ohad to tell me that we were running late. I expected him to keep the container, basically to be "The Man," and get us out on time.

So when I confronted him with this, I remember him saying, "I realized it was late, but you're the New Yorker, you know how long it takes to get around the city. What am I supposed to say?" And I got so furious at him.

I said "Honey, you're supposed to take care of us and you're supposed to let me know what's happening." All these "should have's".

He said "Oh, so you wanted me to create this container. You wanted me to let you know that we were running late. That was my job?"

I remember I got so furious the whole cab ride to the workshop, like "I can't believe you didn't tell me." l was so yearning for him to create the container and the structure so I could relax. I mean not all the time. I'm good at creating my own boundaries when I need to, but in this relationship I really was yearning for him to be more of "The Man," whatever that means.

Since that time I would say he understands what I need as a woman. Now I can't even imagine that happening.

Ohad: As much as it was not fun for me to get her Kali [dark Hindu goddess] or, should I say, her Lilith energy, she was right to call my attention to that topic.

I could have just said, "You know, honey, it is 10:00 a.m. already, are you aware of that? Don't you think we should leave?" Instead I was going by my default of just letting it be and not taking control.

You know, I'm also an Israeli, a Mediterranean person. For me it was more like "Yeah, we might be late. So?" But she was a New Yorker and had a whole different state of mind about time. She felt it was a lack of presence on my part, and she was unfortunately right.

In a love relationship it often takes very little effort to check in instead of checking out. But we men tend to check out so many times. This little effort can change so much in the love dynamics between a man and a woman.

She needs to trust me in order to open, and I do want her openness. So I needed to learn what to do to make her able to trust me more, so she can surrender more into love and shine more.

And it is all about simple presence. From Dawn I learned how lack of presence on the man's side is actually hurting the feminine. Yet most women do not show it on the spot and thus they grow bitter, and the relationship gets toxic.

Dawn was showing me the pain of her feminine not feeling met with masculine presence and I took it in. It changed my life in so many realms.

And she did her own work with her expectations and demands and all the "should haves" on her side of the coin.

Marilyn: **So, Dawn, in your story, we heard how the relationship has changed Ohad. How has the relationship demanded that you change?**

Dawn: My life has changed in every way possible. Here I am living with people in a community, in nature and sharing my daily life. Before, I was living in an urban lifestyle in New York. Ohad and I were coming from different worlds, literally and figuratively. He was coming from the religious world and I was coming from the self-help world.

I've grown so much in this relationship just being really accountable and in such a loving container. At the beginning there were so many times where I'd just want to say, "Okay, enough of this!" But I couldn't because there was something in the genuine, serious way that Ohad responded.

Like, I would go, "Take this," and he would say, "Okay, I'm going to take this. And I'm going to work with it and then I'm going to give it back to you.

We're going to keep on working with it."

In the beginning we had a lot more to clear out so we did more work in the beginning. We really made a commitment very early on that when we had a problem we would look at it separately, and say, "How can I improve our relationship? How can I make a shift?"

It takes a lot to think about being with another human for all these years.

Philip: **So after all these years what's a current challenge?**

Dawn: Sometimes I feel a little jealous and issues come up. I look at that as a chance to learn what the issue for me really is. Where am I closing? Where is it really landing in me? What's behind it?

Jealousy definitely hits me more when I'm feeling less powerful and less strong. The more I'm feeling mopey in my life, the more the other person can invoke jealousy in me. I'm tempted to feel they are more successful.

But I have to say even though I'm sort of a self-protective person, jealous by nature in some way, I've worked through it a lot and it's gotten a lot easier. I see it as a spiritual path.

I chose it. If I didn't, I think I would have thrown up my hands a long time ago. It's too ridiculous, too difficult, too challenging.

Marilyn: **Have you discovered other parts of yourself in being with Ohad, things that have surprised you?**

Dawn: I think the thing that surprised me is how I've gone from being a really active single woman, with always moving and going, into a life where, I don't know...

Some nights I think about going out but I just want to stay in with Ohad and just be in our love field, the love field we're creating. Just enjoying being with each other, it's so nice. So there isn't a yearning outwards as much.

It's funny. My single-woman-very-proud-New-Yorker has faded away, this whole "Ms" thing, this struggling with "me, me, me." and "this is my bank account"...

I feel like I don't have to prove that in my life anymore. I don't have to prove that I'm honored as an individual and as a sacred person.

Philip: **Speaking of sacred, we've been talking so much about the interplay between your spirituality and your love, how they affect each other. Could you give us a story, an example of how this relationship influenced your understanding of Judaism and vice-versa?**

Ohad: What I can say is that our relationship helped me understand, not Judaism, but God. So if Judaism has to do anything with God, you could say that it helped me understand Judaism as well. This relationship has helped me learn not to use my Jewish spirituality to avoid contact and not to go study my books to avoid conflict or to avoid drama.

Dawn was really a great educator, because she helped me see that the real core of things is happening now, in the present moment, just here, between us.

It's not somewhere else, somewhere where there is a dead Rabbi talking through books, but it is here, just in front of me, at this very moment, with a live woman.

Philip: **Okay, Dawn, on your side, what has been your journey with your love and your Jewish spirituality?**

Dawn: It has always been important for me to have someone to share "my Jewish life," to have someone to share rituals with. I always wanted that.

Before I was with Ohad I was engaged to a non-Jewish man, and the first time after I went to services at BJ's (an alternative Jewish, "Gospel-style" synagogue in New York City) I remember crying because God made me fall in love with my religion and a non-Jewish man at the same time. He really was a good man but I was struggling so much with this. When we were trying to plan the wedding we couldn't even decide whether it would be a Rabbi or a Reverend. Ultimately the whole thing just fell apart.

Philip: So you fell in love with Judaism as an adult?

Dawn: You know, I had a very strong awakening as an adult, but as a kid I went to Jewish day school, Jewish summer camps, and B'nai B'rith Youth. I was pretty Jewish. Then in my 20's I was more interested in everything, Hinduism, Native Americanism, Wicca, goddess. Then in my mid-30's I met a Jewish guy! He said, "Would you like to come for a Shabbas dinner?" And I said, "Wow! A Shabbas dinner. That sounds so nerdy and you're so cute! How can that be?" It was so out of my context at that point that there were even cool Jews.

And he told me about these cool synagogues; he said, "I'm going to Carlebach's Shul," and I said, "Okay, I'll come. And there was a *Mechitzah* (men and women sitting in separate sections), but I loved it. I loved the joy. Then he said, "Let's stop by BJ's (B'nai Jeshurun Synagogue), I think you might like it."

	I just remember the music, the joy, it was so luminescent, and my heart just embraced the whole room.
	Since then I was hooked. I went every Friday night. And that was it, I moved from the back of the shul up to the back of the balcony and then to the middle and then to the front. And that was it. I was there. It changed my life.
	And then I met Ohad.
	And of course with him it's not even a question of whether we are practicing a Jewish life. That's who we are. It sources everything we do. But we're living a Judaism that's different, that I couldn't have even imagined before, a Judaism that we call the Hebraic Path. It brings in a lot of the ancient tribal life of Judaism with its pastoral culture and connection to the land, something that both Ohad and I had a common interest in, even before we met. A lot of the spiritual components of our lives before we met have been incorporated into the way we practice our Judaism now. So, like the High Holidays, for instance, we go down to the forest, we do services there. We combine our Judaism with a lot of Sufism and some Native American ways, particularly Lakota. It's Renewal Judaism. It's exciting. Our interests have grown and formed together and we're creating together.
Ohad:	I have a story for you about how my love relationship has influenced my Judaism. I pray a lot but I don't do the regular prayer from the *Siddur* (traditional prayer book) because it usually feels to me like I'm boring God.
Marilyn:	Boring God?
Ohad:	Just kidding, of course. But I don't do the Jewish text anymore in prayer. It doesn't reflect my authenticity and my set of beliefs.

But one time, I went to visit my friends and they were praying the regular prayers. So I said to myself, "Okay. I will just flow with them." The words in the text were not expressing my heart. So what I did was, I intentionally applied my practice of sacred sexuality of how I move, the way I move my body, the way I breathe and the way I open my heart and I applied it all into the prayer.

I remember experiencing a complete spiritual orgasm. It wasn't a bodily orgasm but it was an explosion of the heart and of the consciousness, a complete feeling of wonder and of communion with the divine. It was a real mystical experience just in my friends' apartment, very mundane. I didn't even tell them. Dawn tells me now that I didn't tell her about this experience until several years later.

So you can say that my relationship has helped me understand Judaism, yes.

Dawn: I'm not sure how intimate we want to get. We definitely have stories.

Ohad: The question is how radical you want to go in your book. Our school is a school of love and Kabbalah. We are like Tantra teachers, teachers of conscious sexuality. We deal with it a lot, but for some people it might be over the border.

Dawn: Yeah. We're kind of radical folks.

Ohad: Here's a story. When Dawn had started her period and we were making love. I took her blood – I am an artist – and I painted with it. I painted a lion.

Dawn: Yeah it was beautiful.

Ohad: I felt it's the power of the Feminine. Also, for me, it was a healing for many years of being an Orthodox Rabbi.

	I would be really going away from women's bleeding. I was realizing that this is not right. Respecting is the way and not rejecting. So I took this blood and I made art from it and gave the drawing to Dawn.
Dawn:	A lion roaring. With a red mane. I have it still somewhere. I just remembered how touching it was, how sweet that he really saw me and he honored me in my sacred time. Since then it's been interesting. Now we don't make love, necessarily, when I'm bleeding because then it's the woman's time. It's like a time where he won't come to me but if it's my desire and I ask him, then it's okay. So now, it's the way we do the *Niddah* (The time of ritual separation between spouses when the woman is bleeding).
Ohad:	It's respecting the feminine time.
Marilyn:	I understand. You honor the separation but you put the power of choice into the hands of the woman.
Ohad:	Yeah. It's her time. She can decide if she wants a separation or a sexual connection and to what degree.
Marilyn:	**You talk a lot about sexuality. Would you say that the sexual relationship exists outside the bed too?**
Dawn:	Of course.
Ohad:	Sexuality is not only in bed. It not only has to do with genitals. It's the way we look at each other. From Kabalistic points of view, it's all divine lovemaking whenever the energies are merging. Lovemaking happens in many, many, many ways; sometimes during a family meal.
Philip:	What happens at the dinner table that would make you say "Oh there it is"?

Dawn: It can be as subtle as the way you hand someone the food across the table.

Ohad: It's just sitting with my parents at a family meal and then connecting with Dawn across the table. She's opening to me and my look to her will be penetrating, nothing being said. It's obvious to us and God. No one else sees it, or maybe they do, but they don't know to what degree we are actually connecting right there. For us this is great.

Marilyn: Nice. You guys seem really willing to share a lot of intimacy with us. How do you strike a balance between your public and your private life?

Ohad: With us public and private is tricky because we teach relationships as a couple, so our relationship is out there in some ways but we keep a lot private. We do not keep secrets, so we are open with our lifestyle, and still we keep the intimacy of our life. I think we found a nice balance about it. We definitely have privacy but there's no hiding because of fear or shame. There's no "Oh this is inappropriate. As a Rabbi I shouldn't." My feeling is that, as a Rabbi I should show that I'm a human being, and I'm a loving being, and I'm an erotic being.

And it does not contradict in any way my devotion. In fact, it's the opposite.

Many Rabbis try to create a second persona as if there were a separation between their love life and their rabbinical life. This is weird for me. For us there is no separation.

One of the problems of Judaism today is that Judaism went away from Love and from Eros. It became a kind of Christian Judaism with Rabbis trying to avoid showing themselves as erotic beings. As if, if you're a Rabbi, you have no desires and you are away from sexuality.

I do believe it's quite the opposite. What I feel is important is to bring sacredness and consciousness into the field of love and sexuality.

And if Rabbis could study that and be a healthy model for that, this will help their congregation much more than hiding their relationships and putting a picture of like "Oh, we are a nice Jewish family."

Dawn: For me the public/private balance was a different kind of challenge. I moved from New York to Israel. In the beginning I didn't even have my own life. I didn't have my own friends. So I submerged myself into Ohad's life and his world. And then slowly it became *our* life and *our* world and it wasn't so much *his*. That's still a struggle. I still yearn for my own friends, my own connections, people that are outside our circle. Not that it's so defined who is in our circle. We're not synagogue people per se. But we have people who come for services and rituals and people who come for the school.

We don't make the separation like a lot of synagogue-and-pulpit Rabbis and Rebbetzins do. They live their lives in more defined ways where "This is the way we are in public," and they don't show their private side.

We have a pretty open life. I think we are more transparent. A lot of people know that. But they don't really know until they know. I mean, I feel like a lot of people think they know but they don't really know. And then a lot of people when they get to know us they say, "Oh, so that's you. That's who you really are. Okay, I've heard all these stories." I don't know how to prevent the stories. Once you become a public person, people love to talk.

So we just have our deep friends. And I think we do have a nice bit of private time as well.

	Sometimes, we just shut out the world and say, "Okay, it's me and Ohad, and sometimes, our stepson, celebrating; just us. Sometimes we take a couple of days.
	Sometimes we just say, "Let's just watch a movie tonight and not go out," and it's blessed.
Marilyn:	Interesting, Dawn, how you two went to very different places with this public/private question. Ohad, you seem to be talking about what other people can see and know about your relationship and, Dawn, you are talking about a need to share and process intimate matters with people, special friends outside your immediate circle.
Philip:	And you also talked about the need for private time together. How do you both see your relationship? It's a primary relationship? You're soul-mates? You're married?
Ohad:	All of it. All of the above.
Dawn:	Yes, we are married. We did our own special ceremony, different in some ways from the traditional Jewish wedding so it will reflect our values.
Marilyn:	It seems like before you two met you each had this incredible vision of love. What you've actually created seems beyond what either of you imagined.
Dawn:	I had certain visions, qualities that I wanted in a relationship; deep freedom and yet strong partnership with someone that I could honor, and respect, and love, a good love-making partner, a fun person to be with and I got it all. I'd always dreamed of a love like this but somehow I never believed it possible. I really count it as a blessing.
Ohad:	Really we were just dreaming each other up.

Ohad and Dawn are the creators of KabaLove. They say, "In its true meaning KabaLove is a path of devotion. It is an ongoing practice of serving God in love through and via love to your intimate partner." **http://eng.kabalove.org**

Rabbi Ohad and Dawn
The Blue Thread in their Love Story

And then both men and women will be gentle.
And then both women and men will be strong.
And then no person will be subject to another's will.
And then all will be rich and free and varied....
And then everywhere will be called Eden once again.
  -- Judy Chicago. From The Merger Poem
(Sometimes this poem is used in Jewish Liturgy as Aleynu Leshabeyach)

Lilith, the archetype of the strong sexual woman in Jewish mythology, is alone and condemned to be so because she "refused to lie under Adam." What message does this send to women? And also, to men?

How can a man be with a woman when that woman is in her full power? And what is it like for a woman to be in a partnership where she is fully accepted in all her power, sexual and otherwise?

As a man, and as a scholar, and as a Rabbi, Ohad wrote a book about Lilith calling for a fresh way to think about her and her radical relationship, both to the penis and also to the man behind it. Instead of condemning, suppressing, or fearing the Lilith-like attributes in his partner, he has to welcome them. He has to face what he calls, "The Power of the Feminine."

Ohad: *I prayed to God like "Please show me how do I deal with this, Power of the Feminine." ... It feels really dangerous ... I guess with many men the big fear is feminine emotions, women and emotions, like war is less frightening.*

Ohad's claim is that a man pays a price when he refuses to allow the women in his life to be as independent, self-empowered, passionate and sexual as she is capable of being. He diminishes his own spiritual potential. Men, if you want to be as full as you can be, you have to want her to be as full as she can be.

In his relationship with Dawn, he acknowledges his fears, gets to overcome them, and then gets to feel solid and spiritually present.

> *Ohad:* *Dawn ... helped me see that the real core of things is happening now, in the present moment, just here, between us. It's not somewhere else, somewhere where there is a dead Rabbi talking through books, but it is here, just in front of me, at this very moment, with a live woman.*

And on her side, she is surprised to find herself less in need to prove something about herself, even more peaceful. It's a very surprising outcome for both of them.

> *Dawn:* *It's funny. My single-woman-very-proud-New-Yorker has faded away, this whole "Ms" thing, this struggling with "me, me, me." and "this is my bank account"... I feel like I don't have to prove that in my life anymore. I don't have to prove that I'm honored as an individual and as a sacred person.*

For us, this is the blue thread in their story, a call to men and women to fully encounter each other.

Some might say, "Treat each other as equals." That would miss a lot. There is a fine line here. The idea of being equals can be as rigid as the idea of one person always being on top. Lilith didn't refuse to *ever* lie under Adam. She just didn't want to *always* do it. In Dawn and Ohad's vision the woman gets to lead sometimes or follow sometimes, depending on what's needed. Look at how Ohad and Dawn re-invent the *Niddah* ritual. In their version the man still cannot approach her but, if she wants, she can approach him. It's her decision. For some Jews this would be a *shanda* (scandal). But, as Dawn and Ohad said, they are radical folks, "sometimes over the border."

There was much about their teaching that was radical and challenging. In this book nine couples have shared their stories about what happens between them on the path of Love. They all referred to their lovemaking, but obliquely. Only Dawn and Ohad talk about their lovemaking explicitly.

As we listened to Dawn and Ohad we were once again huddled with that young Talmudic student under his Rabbi's bed spying on what Leibish so delicately called their "marital intimacy." Do we really need to know what happens when spiritual people take their clothes off, get in bed, touch each others' public and private parts, i.e., make love? But, of course, that's why the story was in the Talmud in the first place. "This, too, is Torah we really need to learn."

If we really want to understand the spiritual dimension of marriage, then earthly love, physical love, gets its own blue thread.

Loving couples make love often and with pleasure and joy. For them sex is a celebration. Ohad and Dawn are explicit about their sex lives.

They want to remind us that physical lovemaking (yes that) is an important spiritual experience, a tangible way to experience the Presence of God.

Dawn: *There was always a quality of sacredness in our lovemaking, of really setting a prayer, an intention to make Love. Sometimes we felt like, "How can I contain all this pleasure? It feels selfish almost." And, so through our lovemaking, we started sending it out as a prayer to the people in our lives. It became so potent that it became one of our ways of praying.*

People cry out "Oh God Oh God," in their intimate moments. Ohad and Dawn ask us to take those spontaneous cries seriously. They say that lovemaking is a form of prayer and prayer is a form of love-making.

Ohad: *[I was praying with friends and] I applied my practice of sacred sexuality of how ... I move – the way I move my pelvis and the way I move my body and the way I breath and the way I open my heart intentionally. ... And I remember experiencing a complete spiritual orgasm.*

It wasn't a bodily orgasm but it was like really like an explosion of the heart and of the consciousness and ... a complete feeling of wonder.

When two people really open up to each other, when every touch is also a prayer, when they meet in a realm beyond words, God is there to greet them. This land beyond words is a tangible spiritual reality. There are spiritual traditions that say that the way to know God is by shutting down the distraction of sensuality. Ohad and Dawn describe a very different path.

But this takes us to perhaps the most challenging part of their story. Dawn and Ohad have made a deliberate and intentional commitment to non-monogamy. How

does this fit into a book about spirituality and love relationships? Can a non-monogamous relationship be considered sacred? We both argued back and forth about this for a long time.

For Marilyn something sacred must be done with consciousness, integrity, intentionality, and mutual respect and can't intentionally harm the other. Although she has seen examples of non-monogamy that don't meet those standards, with Ohad and Dawn, it is sacred. Dawn is the first to say, "It's not for everybody" but for them it is a spiritual practice and Dawn talks about using the jealousy that comes up to face her own insecurities.

Marilyn admires the courage of Ohad and Dawn to break with conventionality, in order to follow their own integrity, their own path and not just follow rules for the sake of simplicity and acceptance.

For Philip, it's not so much about sacredness but about intimacy. He can see how, through non-monogamy, Ohad and Dawn will discover things about sex, love, and spirituality that monogamous couples will never know. At the same time, though, he believes that monogamous couples will experience things about intimacy that a non-monogamous couple will not.

In many non-monogamous partnerships partners have deeply personal, private moments that can't be shared. One can't explore both paths at the same time. One has to choose.

Where we agreed is that the main thing is that both partners know what they are dealing with. What is clearly not sacred, or intimate, is the pretense of monogamy, with secrets and lies. What Ohad and Dawn are doing clearly demonstrates one of their moral principles: in creating a relationship, choices must be made and made equally and openly by both partners.

Dawn and Ohad are creating a new paradigm. Their vision of Judaism, "The Hebraic Path," harkens back to Genesis, the Beginning, where "Male and Female created He them." The vision of Adam and Lilith in the Garden captures some of it. They've named their ashram, "The Garden," a place where, "*Both men and women will be gentle. Both women and men will be strong. ... And then everywhere will be called Eden once again.*"

Chapter Seven
Two Rabbis, One Soul

Rabbi Victor and Nadya Gross

We are different people. And the beauty of our work together is that we've learned how to do that dance. We really mirror one another, where we bring opposite attributes or experiences into the relationship. We teach that what seems to be the opposite in your partner is what grounds you and completes you. – Nadya Gross

We came to the realization that it's not about a perfect relationship, even if it was achievable. The excitement, the engagement, is in the perfecting. – Victor Gross

The next messiah will be a couple. This is the premise which inspired this book. Victor and Nadya got there years before we did and lived according to this premise. He is a Rabbi. She is a Rabbi. But they have been ordained as *one* Rabbi by Reb Zalman who affectionately calls them Neshama Achat (One Soul). They are the first, and so far the only, Rabbinical couple ordained in this way. Two people, one soul. What can we learn from their journey?

Philip: **So, Victor, Nadya, tell us your story about how it all began. You probably have different stories.**

Victor: I'm a trained historian. So I'm familiar with multiple narratives but, Nadya, you begin. Yours is much more exciting than mine.

Nadya: When we met, I was a senior in high school, 16 years old. Victor had just come to Los Angeles fresh out of seminary and he was 25. And he went to work for United Synagogue Youth, a Jewish youth organization that I was a member of.

The first event he came to was a weekend retreat in California. I'm from Israel. I had come to the United States when I was 12 years old and one of the counselors had asked me if I'd like to meet somebody just back from Israel. I thought he was introducing me to an Israeli, and I went along.

When I was introduced to Victor, there was an immediate knowing that I had. I have always seen things.

Always through my childhood I saw things that other people didn't see. But when I came to the United States, I shut that off, I stopped seeing. And in that moment that I was introduced to Victor it all came back. I saw an incredible ray of light that went from my third eye to Victor's heart. And in that ray of light I saw all the past lives that we'd had together and I knew in that moment that this was the person that I was supposed to meet in this lifetime and continue the stories that we have been creating for a long, long time.

And I was not looking to be intimately involved with anybody at that point in my life. I had other plans for myself that did not involve a relationship with somebody and certainly not one that was going to define the rest of my life. But I couldn't deny what I saw.

Marilyn:	So you knew. What did you do with that knowing?
Nadya:	Well, I didn't do anything in that moment because I hadn't been seeing like that for many years. I had to deal with what that was all about. I didn't want to say anything to anybody until I checked in with my grandmother. She had been my mentor and had helped me make sense of that seeing when I was a child.
	You know, you can see things that tell you this is what you're supposed to do with your life but you still have free choice.
	So meanwhile I spent a lot of time deciding if I was going to follow that path or turn my back on it and do the things I thought I was going to do.
	So when we first met, that was Thanksgiving weekend of 1971. Oh my God! That was like forever ago! But for the rest of that school year, I had to figure out a way to convince him that I wasn't as young as I looked.
	We didn't make a personal connection until Spring. Then I actually surrendered to it and asked him to take me to my senior prom. Yeah. Yeah. I invited him on our first date. So it's a little funny now when I think about it. And of course our children think it's totally ridiculous. But it's my story and I'm sticking to it.
Philip:	Remind me again, how old were you?
Nadya:	I was 16.
Victor:	And I was 25. At that time I was kind of still a hippy. When she asked me to take her to the senior prom, it cost me all sorts of angst. I didn't even go to my own senior prom. I told her I would call her.
	That night, at the synagogue Reb Shlomo Carlebach was giving a concert. I was talking to him backstage and I looked at my watch and I said, "Oy. I gotta go call a woman."

And he said, "If I had to choose between either talking to me or talking to a woman, I'd talk to the woman."

So I went off to talk on the phone with Nadya, and Shlomo was playing his music in the background. Who knows how much of that was coming through. It's only much later that I realized Shlomo had such an effect on me.

Then after the prom, she was going to Israel in the summer and I was returning to Israel. So we agreed to make up.

Nadya: Meet up.

Victor: Meet up. Well that was Freudian.

So in Israel I went and rented a motor scooter. And we traveled all over the country. And it was driving down into the valley near Jerusalem at a high speed on a motor scooter when I said in my typical way, "I think I'm in love with you."

Nadya: Yeah. So it took from when we met in November until that summer for him to come around.

Victor: Yes.

Nadya: But I was there all along.

Victor: Yeah. And the strangest thing was that in that initial period it was so comfortable.

It was so different. There was never anything problematic. I used to scratch my head privately wondering what this meant. It wasn't superficial. It was getting deeper and deeper, you know, our exploration of who we were.

And there weren't any of those moments where you say, "I don't know. I have to get over this challenge or it won't work." It was never that in that initial period of time ... only later.

Philip: What came up later? The age difference?

Victor: As far as the age difference went, my friends thought I was crazy. They questioned the correctness of it.

	That was the early seventies. At that time we didn't question the ethics of it. If it was happening today it would be different. I recently wrote an ethics code for our Rabbinic association which stated that what I did was a no-no. It was a different time.
	Nadya can speak to how she felt about being in a relationship with someone older and more experienced. For me it was a soul connection. I know that now; I didn't then.
Marilyn	I'm curious about something. Did that request to go to the senior prom come out of the blue? Was Victor shocked?
Nadya:	Victor was. Victor was staff advisor to the USY Board I was on. In January I started working with him mostly on the telephone. But to him I was just another one of the kids. I realized I had to make myself visible to him.
	I would try to get his advice on things, things I didn't even need his advice for but it was a way of talking to him. Victor was this brilliant mind so I knew that I had to play to that and get him to notice that I wasn't just one of the kids, I was smarter.
	By February I had already told my mother that I'd met the guy I was going to marry and we still hadn't even seen each other; I was still just talking to him on the phone.
	Then, in April just before my birthday, I asked him on the telephone if he would take me to my senior prom. I don't even know how I worked up the gumption to do it. He was supposed to be my mentor and I just, kind of, asked him. And he told me he'd have to think about it. But I knew he would take me to my prom. I already told my mother he was going to and I went and bought my dress.
Marilyn:	You bought your dress?

Nadya: Because I just knew it. There was absolute certainty because this was the way it was supposed to be. It wasn't a question of playing games. I was just going on what I knew was true. And if I knew it, it was going to become known to him at some point in some way.

Philip: So when you told your mom, "This is the man I'm going to marry," did she believe you?

Nadya: Well, I think my mother probably hoped I would get over it. The grandmother that I spoke of, my father's mother, she knew. But she was the only one I could tell the truth to. My mother just believed that I had some wild crush. And because I told her he was taking me to my prom, she invited him to this surprise birthday party she was making for me.

And Victor told me later that he accepted the invitation to the birthday party because he needed to remember what I looked like before he decided that he would take me to my prom.

That's all the impression that I had made on him up to that time. And so, he drove out to my birthday party and then decided, I guess, that I had the right kind of look for him to take me to this senior prom.

Victor: Now, if you want to take from, say, the Greek Agape and Eros, I was not in the Agape, I'll assure you. I was much more into Eros at the time. Right? So I will admit that my initial attraction was the physical world.

Nadya: So it wasn't a lot of contact. We certainly weren't being friends. But I kept finding reasons to engage with him. I kept stoking the fire that way.

Victor: It's gotten better and deeper.

Marilyn: You hinted that the challenges came later.

Victor: I would say for the very first number of years we kind of coasted. Or I coasted on the ease of the relationship. It was easy. Nadya was in college and I worked in Synagogues. It was that wonderful mid-70's student life. There was no focus on the relationship.

In '78 we moved to Israel which was an enormous challenge. Then came the birth of our first son. It was about 1980 when I came to the realization that our relationship was at stake.

I became aware that I was dissociating more and more from the relationship. I had become more self-centered. What did I really want to do in life? Who was I? I didn't disassociate from the love and care of our child. But frankly I would say that Nadya took a back seat.

But then there was a realization. I remember the moment and I remember the clarity. If you were to use a spiritual term, it was a revelation.

We were in Los Angeles. It was 1982. I was in the living room of our house. The physical experience of it was like, I was in this fog encapsulating me and then suddenly it cleared out. There was just this cleanliness in my mind as the feelings and the thoughts all came together in that moment. I was standing facing Nadya and it just flowed through me, in me. It just poured out of me. I realized that I was truly, deeply, completely in love with Nadya and that my life and its meaning was surrounded by her being in my life as my lover, my partner, my friend. And I said it.

I'm not sure what would have happened if she had not been, at that moment, standing across from me. I needed her presence. And it was a presence that was beyond physical.

Later, when we became deeply involved in Kabbalah we understood that it was really the top three *Sefirot, Chabad: Chochmah, Binah* and *Da'at.*

	And at that moment they came together and that was it. It was a tautology of knowing. Now, I can understand it.
Marilyn:	How did Nadya react when you told her that?
Victor:	She agreed.
Marilyn:	What did she agree with?
Victor:	Relationship is a spiritual practice, as she likes to put it. It has to be worked on 24/7. I began to realize that it's not just 24/7 that you're working at the relationship, but that it's being aware of it 24/7. I need to always be aware of my relationship whether she's sitting next to me or whether she is somewhere else in the world.
	And you have to have triggers to remind you because it's so easy to fall out of that consciousness.
	For me the solution became to make no differentiation between my mental engagement with her and my feeling engagement with her. I began to realize that my whole being was invested in this relationship.
	We didn't just slough off my realization, my vision in the living room, as a mere revelatory moment. We began at this date to take it seriously and do the work.
Nadya:	First of all you have to understand I came to our relationship as a child. Really. And I had to grow up in that relationship. Also, I'd been kind of unconscious since I came to the United States. I had forgotten what I'd been taught. The couple of years that we went to live in Israel we were reunited with my grandmother who was my mentor. All of these things came alive in me once again. That was really important.
	And so, for me, the challenge was how much of the change and transformation going on in me could I reveal without pushing him away or without scaring him away.

I grew up as a mystic, my grandmother was a mystic. Victor was trained as a rationalist. So I grew up in a very different kind of world view. And I played his head game really well. As I said when I was trying to get his attention, I could meet him in that place of the intellect but it wasn't where I really lived.

So that was my big challenge as I was coming into my adulthood and reclaiming my spirituality and my sight. It was how much to reveal of myself. How could I trust that Victor would really understand who I really was? How do I reveal it in a way that he can embrace my becoming?

So, when we first came back to the States I got us to be initiated in transcendental meditation. Then I could meditate and I could tell him that I had these insights in my meditation which were really old stories that I just needed to start revealing. Stuff that I knew was true all along. But now it was like, "Oh, in my meditation I had this vision, right?"

Also at the same time I went and trained as a past-life-regression therapist. It was a lark and some of my friends were doing it.

Victor had a lot of anxiety about me playing in those realms. And he would find all kinds of admonitions from our tradition against witches and so on from his rational training. And every time he would try to warn me in that way, I would feel that I had to hide again.

So I would say that there was tension and disconnection. Before his revelation, when Victor talked about being more selfish or more self-referencing, what I was feeling was that he couldn't know me for who I really was.

I was trying to reveal a little bit, in what I thought were safe ways, about my training and my upbringing.

So there was distancing that would happen between us and it was very painful.

And this went on maybe two years when we first came back to the States. I was seeking validation and relationships with people who I could talk to about these things. And we had different friends all of a sudden. We had different experiences with people that were igniting us. And that was scary.

It was in a moment when either one of us could have just said, "There's such a distance here that we could walk away." Or we could realize, there was something important here that had to be preserved.

Well, I knew I couldn't walk away. I'm sure I played with the idea. What would it be like to not be in the struggle?

But at the same time that original vision had never ever left me, that sense that this is really my soul mate, the person, the soul with which I've been in relationship for many, many lifetimes. And we have work to do together and it's really beautiful that we are together.

Philip: **So there was a great distance and also a great longing. And through it all you knew you were soul mates. What about Victor?**

Nadya: I think that what I did was create an image for him of what a wasteland life would be if we weren't together.

Philip: How did you do that?

Nadya: By allowing – by allowing that wasteland to come into full relief, by not engaging, by not being as emotionally available and present to him as I had always been.

Philip: It was a strategy?

Nadya: I can't give myself credit for being that conscious yet.

	So it was more – it was more of this sort of painful reality that was emerging in our lives that I was feeding.
Philip:	And this was before his realization in the living room?
Nadya:	Yeah.
Philip:	Victor, did you know that she was feeling so separate from you?
Victor.	Yes. I felt impotent because I didn't know how. I didn't know how to win her back. And I didn't know how to present my emerging self while at the same time acknowledging the importance of the relationship. There was that period of great confusion.
Nadya:	And I just wanted him to get out of his head and drop into his heart. His head told him that those visions that I had and the things I believed in were not okay. The things I was into scared him. They were forbidden. They were no-no's.
	So a part of me was speaking to his heart and another part of me was really feeding that wasteland because I wasn't feeling met. I was hiding. I was always really good at hiding. Because all my life, that training that I received from my grandmother was all secrets. I was really good at keeping those secrets and being hidden.
	And also, I wasn't trusting that he would be able to, or even willing, to meet me.
	And then he had his moment.
Philip:	So how many years has it been since that breakthrough?
Nadya:	Oh, that was in the early '80s.
Victor:	And we've been – we've been doing the work ever since.

Marilyn: **So what would you say if you had to name a challenge in the relationship today, a current challenge?**

Nadya: For me I would say that it's a more updated, and certainly a much more evolved.

But still some remnant of, that distinction between the two of us. Victor is still very rational in his thinking even though he's learned how to live in his heart big time. And he's a cynic and he's a historian and he believes that history repeats itself. I still see a very different kind of picture and believe unequivocally in the capacity of humanity to transform itself.

So just today we had an encounter that was painful because we see things going on in the Middle East very differently. And whenever those conversations come up, it's really hard because I really admire and respect and understand where Victor is coming from. But I just want him to open to another perspective. I'll let him say what he really feels but I feel that he gets upset with me because my perspective maybe sounds naïve, or unrealistic.

This is probably the only instance that I can think of in our lives right now where we are really divided but I'm usually silent. I usually don't choose to engage about those things. And when I do, you know, it's hard for him and for me. Most of the time I just witness Victor's strong feelings and I try not to engage.

We are different people. And the beauty of our work together is that we've learned how to do that dance. We've learned how to dance where we really mirror one another, where we bring opposite attributes or experiences into the relationship.

A lot of what we teach is about appreciating how what seems to be the opposite in your partner is what grounds you.

	It grounds you and completes you. Whatever it is that we're teaching together we're able to do that dance very, very fluidly, and we're very beautiful.

And I think that this [disagreement about the current crisis in the Middle East] isn't just the only place we have to deal with this. It's because I have wounding around this that it creates for me a problem. I have a lot of wounding around my feelings about my country and my voice about that which has been mostly stifled. So that's my issue.

Philip: Yeah. It seems like the issue of you knowing something in your heart and then not saying, goes all the way back to your very beginning story.

Nadya: That's true. It's too – it's too precious.

Victor: And when those things come up, it kind of, in a small way it soils the relationship for that moment because, for me, it's an intellectual engagement. And it wouldn't matter if it was somebody I knew or didn't know. It's like I'm sitting on a forum and I don't know the person. And for that moment, there is kind of soiling of my love for Nadya.

And more and more now I rein myself in. I give myself a message, "Don't go off so much because it's not worth it. There isn't that much at stake." And I'm getting better at not just scoring debate points.

I was trained that way. I studied all of those years of Talmud, you know. And so, getting out of that has always been a challenge.

I thought that the goal was to experience the perfect relationship. And then we came to the realization that it's not about a perfect relationship, even if it was achievable. The excitement, the engagement, is in the perfecting.

	Every year on our anniversary we spend the first part of the day doing our *Tshuvah* (restoring) work with each other. When we first started doing it, however long ago it was, it took up a good part of the day. We had a lot of *Tshuvah* to do.
Philip:	To those of us who don't know, what does that exactly mean?
Victor:	It's reformatting and recalibrating the fine points of our relationship for that year. Asking, "What is it that needs a little tinkering with?"

For instance, this is one of the things that Nadya said to me this year: Our desks are right next to each other but I have the ability particularly when I'm studying or working to go so deep that I'm unaware.

And so Nadya brought that up. "Can you just stop every so often and reconnect?" She wanted me to get up and go over and give her whatever to let her know that I'm conscious that she's there and we're in relationship. It's not like I am a total failure at that. But there are those times that I'm lost in my own world.

Nadya: And out of that loss of consciousness comes sort of an imposition of self, like, suddenly he wants to tell me something or read something to me and he's not even aware that I may be deeply engaged in something and remember to just say, "Hey, do you have a minute?" Or "Can I share something with you right now?"

For me, the practice of always being aware of our relationship is part of my self-definition. There's always an aspect of myself that is tuned in to who he is, where he is, what he is about. And I know when he's lost that thread on his end. So there needs to be an attunement.

Marilyn: So basically, that's your nature and you're always tuned into him and you're trying to get Victor to be just as tuned in to you?

Nadya: I have – I have an acute empathic sense. Some of that is not trainable. It's more on the level of just being aware that there's someone besides yourself who may have needs, interests, obligations whatever at any particular moment. And so when you want to engage with that person, you have to take that first step of checking in.

But also, when Victor completely disconnects, as he can, he imagines that I've disconnected. So what I do want him to work at is understanding that his disconnect is not my disconnect. Right? Because then he can create a story for himself that I haven't been available. He can start to feel like, "Where am I?" which causes angst for him.

Victor: I'm not even conscious of myself most of the time. I can be studying a Hassidic text and get into that spiritual world of whatever it is. If I'm studying a period of Jewish history in preparation for the class I'm teaching, then I'm in that period. I'm not here in this world now. And then when I come out of it, I suddenly go, "Well, where is she?" I mean, she's there but she's not there.

Nadya: It is truly amazing.

So to be fair to Victor, there are things that Victor has to ask of me as well. So when we do our work together now it's more about asking for support, or awareness or witnessing each other at our growing edge.

So Victor is a very passionate human being. He's passionate about everything even about scoring debate points. On the other hand, I keep that side of me under wraps, partly because there's this stuff inside of me that's really precious. And he really needs me to be more passionate, more expressive of that passion and I'm working on it.

Philip: Interesting. You said earlier that he was more in his head than his heart.

Marilyn: But I hear passion as some place other than the head or the heart, is that right?

Victor: Yeah. There was this philosopher Maimonides, and he was a misogynist, but he said, the difference between men and women is that, for men, passion comes through his head and into his heart and for women, he said, it comes down into the heart and then flows up into the mind. I find that utter nonsense, all right, because it works for me very differently.

I'm just – I am – I am – and I think Nadya will acknowledge it, I'm passionately in love with her. I mean, it's 41 years we've known each other. The passion hasn't... it's still fire, right?

And I express it in all sorts of ways, verbally, physically. I admit I want it returned in the same measure, even though I know that it's not a realistic expectation. It's just well, gee, what would happen if the flames were this high, if hers were this high, then it would be up that high.

There are so many Yin and Yang things about us. Sometimes my passion is over the top and I'm not aware of it and I need to temper it.

There are other times, when her passion is up tempo from what I am used to, and then it's a delight.

Marilyn: The passion is not just about the love, right? You're also passionate about ideas.

Nadya: His passion – he's so invested in whatever he believes is true or right, whatever he, you know – yeah, whatever he's committed to, whether it's ideas or practices or anti-practices, he's so very passionate, very fiery.

	My stuff runs deeper or runs into depths that doesn't always erupt in that way, right? And that's part of the dance.
	It's a beautiful dance that we get to do because they're actually, they're not opposite. They're mirroring. They mirror each other. Plus it's another way of expressing the same thing.
Philip:	That's beautiful. That's beautiful.
Marilyn:	**Victor, what would you give as an example of the current challenge of the relationship?**
Victor:	So for most of the years, the age difference disappeared. Now, it's taken a different form but it's there. Reb Zalman wrote a book, "From Aging to Saging." I'm doing that work because I'm in that period of my life and Nadya is conscious of it. And we both teach it and yet, I feel it and this is a reverse role now. She intellectualizes it for the most part but she knows I'm going through it. She knows she will go through it maybe nine years from now when I will be really old, so to speak.
Philip:	What is your age right now?
Victor:	I'll be 67 in February. So it's a whole new stage in my life. I'm doing a lot of the work internally
	and that's a challenge for Nadya to understand and to not just understand but to engage in it, in whatever way she needs to, in relationship with me, and I can't define that.
Philip:	Yeah, because you're not 60 yet, right?
Nadya:	No, I'm 57.
	So – yeah. My body tells me I'm getting older whether I like it or not. It's not intellectual for me. And we have four children spread over 15 and a half years and just now for the first time in 34 years, we have an empty nest. Our baby just went off to college.

So this is a big transition. I've always been in an older world than my age cohort, in part because of Victor and in part because of the work I have chosen to do with my life.

So I have that sense of the shifts that are going on around me and I can notice in myself the shift that's happening.

I think that a big issue right now for us is that Victor is really in a place where he wants to consolidate and focus and retire from something. He wants to do a little bit less and be more focused and have more downtime, which I think is a natural part of the rhythm of life for him. I'm still in producing mode and creating new programs.

We've always worked together as a team. Do I just go ahead and do these things and we don't do them as a team? Or do I temper what I'm doing? Do I focus only on projects we can do as a team? Do I let somebody else do those other projects? I don't have to do them.

Philip: A lot of implications here for both of you.

Nadya: And that means tension for both. But we talk about it. It's not like back in the 80's, when the tension was happening and neither one of us could articulate what was going on. We've learned how to really examine this and really discern what's important here. How do we make these decisions as a team even if the decision we make is that we won't do this as a team? It's a decision that we come to together.

And I feel like I want to support Victor in his desire and his need to slow down, but I would like to think that the way I support him in slowing down is to do a little bit more and pick up the slack. But he'd like me to slow down with him.

Philip: A new phase of life is a real challenge. But this time you're far more skilled at how to work on the relationship.

Marilyn: **Nadya, you talked about the part of you that wants to hide. And yet, you're taking your relationship and offering it to the world in a very public way. So how do you and Victor balance that private world and that public world?**

Nadya: It's funny. I want to say that sometimes Victor is much more revealing than I am and he tells stories that I wish he wouldn't. There are intimacies that to me are very, very private and very deep. At the same time, I feel that our relationship, the fact of our commitment to each other and our love is really what fuels everything we do, and that is completely open to the world. That we completely reveal.

Victor likes to talk about it more, wants to tell the stories and I really believe that it's just so obvious. As a couple they just see the love, it's so palpable. So I say to him, see, we don't have to tell the stories for them.

According to the Kabbalah I received through my grandmother, what caused creation to begin to unfold, was God's longing to be in relationship. By the way that we engage in relationships with our beloved, our family members, our friends, and our neighbors, that is how we step up to that longing of God's.

I would rather teach it through the God language than by revealing some of the intimacies between myself and my beloved here. Frankly I think that in true relationships of intimacy, it's okay that some things are exclusive.

But the fact that we are and that our love is really at the heart of what we are, that's totally available to people and we're totally happy to guide people into that kind of awareness.

When we work with couples who come to us to get married, we won't work with a couple for less than six months.

	I do a whole process with them around relationship as spiritual practice. It's not enough to just be really in love with each other and that love will conquer all. We know that that's untrue.
Marilyn:	Victor, do you have anything to say on that?
Victor:	I would say that finding the language for talk about intimacy took us a long time. How do you get beyond just the feelings? Rev Zalman asked us to write what he called…
Nadya:	Kabbalistic pillow talk.
Victor:	Kabbalistic pillow talk. He'd started it with a few pages years ago and he told us to continue the work. So that's where the thing is. So in other words, my version would be X-rated and Nadya would like for it to be PG.
Marilyn	**Your Judaism and your relationship are very intertwined. Can you both share more about how they influence each other?**
Victor:	From the work I've done with my wife as a Rabbi over 35 years, with marriages and Bar and Bat Mitzvahs, what I've come to realize is that Judaism is all about relationships. Biblical narratives are about relationships, bad ones and good ones. Thank, God, the Bible has both.
	And it's refracted through my understanding and the experience of our relationship.
	But it's so hard for me to say how my relationship shapes my understanding of Judaism because part of the definition of who I am has to do with every aspect of Judaism you can name. I have the trauma of the Jewish people in me.
Nadya:	Part of this whole relationship picture and of our Judaism, is our four children. Our commitment to Judaism in Jewish practice has been well tested by our children.

Our kids very much reflect the sociological realities of today. They've also been raised in a home that gave them permission to find their own path. And that feels very, very important. What does our Jewish practice look like? It's a good testing ground. Can we walk our talk? Do we believe the things that we say we believe?

And how does that inform our relationship with our children? Our four kids always had to share us with the community and they had to be part of the community. They had no choice.

A lot of people felt they had as much of a right to our love and attention as our kids had but we always put our kids first. We don't think that anyone is entitled to us as much as our children are and yet we still have to be very available.

So that's been a big part of our Jewish identity. Our definition of ourselves as Jews has really changed and evolved together.

Victor — Here's one story. One of our kids wanted to play Little League Baseball and they played on Saturday. He would have been very disappointed if we weren't at the game andwe had to lead services.

So when those games were before services started, we were at the game. That changed what we thought Shabbat was supposed to be. But, you know, in my mind, I never – I mean, I remember it - I never wanted him to become an adult and have to do therapy over the fact that his dad missed a baseball game. It became primary.

And tough luck to God and all those people that said that wasn't the right thing to do. It was the right thing to do. Alright? I'm proud that I made that decision. It's not just that it is the right decision. I'm proud that I made that decision.

Nadya: When I met Victor, he had just come to California from a seminary and his year in the seminary was painful and traumatizing. And for the first many years that we were together, he was – he was exorcising the demons of those years. So I heard all his horrendous stories. I had just become really enamored of Jewish practice. I came from a secular Israeli family with a mystical worldview.

It was only by going to a synagogue that I could find people that I could relate with at least with some part of my story.

So I immersed myself in religious practice. I was observing Shabbat and *Kashrut* (Kosher laws) and, you know, all those things that were not issues in my family of origin.

And, Victor, in exorcising the demons was pulling away more from that absolute, you know, requirement of Halachic practice.

I was really into observing all of holidays and Victor had completely dissociated from *Tisha B'Av* which is the day of mourning in the summer time when we mourn the destruction of the temple. He refused to sit on the floor with candles. So I gave it up. I gave it up for many, many years.

And Victor was really my teacher in many ways in those early years Jewishly. He was much more learned than I. And then – and then we came into Jewish renewal and we found ourselves teaching one summer at *Elat Chayyim*, the renewal retreat center.

We were going to be there on *Tisha B'Av* and we were asked to lead the service on the morning of *Tisha B'Av*.

It was quite amazing. What happened was, we had to come up with a way to lead that service that had integrity for both of us. And so we were really able to come to *Tisha B'Av*, not from the historic perspective, but to really understand it as an opportunity for us to get in touch with our own wounding, the things that we mourn, our losses in our lives. And then we can begin to rebuild as the day moves toward the birth of *Moshiach*.

Victor: I feel much more balanced in being a Jew now than ever. I'm comfortable with who I am in relationship to my personal practice, my Judaism and the Jewish people.

It took a long time to do that. Mysticism tempers my reliance on rationality and that's important because it causes me to move away from the exclusive reliance on my training as a rational thinker.

Nadya: I had wanted to go Rabbinical school way back in the day just before I met Victor. There weren't women in the Conservative Movement in those days; they weren't ordaining women. Instead I trained to be a cantor. In the early years of Victor's pulpit work I was the cantor and he was the Rabbi and it worked beautifully.

But as our relationship grew, we started both teaching together and developing things together and it wasn't like the Rabbi talks, the cantor sings. So when we came into Rev Zalman's orbit in Jewish Renewal,

Victor said to me, "Now it's your turn to be a Rabbi." What we came to together was a desire to have our relationship recognized in a new way, our working relationship and our spiritual relationship and our commitment to what we do with others and to what we do between ourselves. It was a new paradigm of Rabbi-ing.

So we asked Rev Zalman to ordain us jointly and after a period of study, our ordination that we received is the joint Rabbinic ordination. To this day Rev Zalman calls us *Neshama Achat* which means one soul. It was meant to be a new paradigm of leadership and also an ordaining of our relationship at the same time.

In the early years of email, when you had to – you know, and in those days we had one computer and so we shared one email,

our email address was oneNeshama@... whatever the domain was, and that's what Rev Zalman came to know us as.

Marilyn: Has Zalman given that to anyone else?
Nadya: We're it.
Victor: We're it.

Rabbi Victor-and-Nadya Gross are the Rabbi at Pardes Levavot, a Jewish Renewal Congregation in Boulder, Colorado.
http://www.pardeslevavot.org

Rabbi Victor-and-Nadya
The Blue Thread in Their Love Story

> *A soul's heavenly source has male and female halves, which are incarnated into the world as a man and a woman. ... This becomes most clear when it comes time for marriage.* The Holy Zohar (1, 55b; 3, 24a)

Sometimes when two notes are sung, a third note emerges from the harmony. It's the same thing that happens in human life. When teams work together well, after a while a sense of the team emerges and players come to see, know and love the team more than they love the individuals on it.

So it is with a love relationship. A sense of the relationship as it's own being emerges and becomes visible to the partners. They start to see how the two of them make one soul. And if the fit is beautiful, it feels as if they were always one soul. When partners in an intimate relationship love the relationship as much as or even more than each other magic happens. A more complex kind of love emerges. For this one soul to emerge, as in harmony singing, there must be two distinct voices.

So often in our discussions of these interviews we end up relating in a way that bears a strange, almost uncanny, resemblance to the very issues the couple in question struggles with.

For some reason, after this interview we felt we had to write about the blue thread in two separate voices. Go figure.

Our disagreement started with our understanding of what Nadya meant by "seeing."

> *Nadya:* When I was introduced to Victor, there was an immediate knowing that I had. I have always seen things. Always through my childhood I saw things that other people didn't see. But when I came to the United States, I shut that off, I stopped seeing. And in that moment that I was introduced to Victor it all came back.

I saw an incredible ray of light that went from my third eye to Victor's heart. And in that ray of light I saw all the past lives that we'd had together. And I knew in that moment that this was the person that I was supposed to meet in this lifetime and continue the stories that we have been creating for a long, long time.

Marilyn: I totally accept Nadya's ability to "see." I accept what she says, that she has an ability to see into the past and into the future. For me it is more than mere intuition; it is a deep knowing. She trusts her clairvoyance totally. What she doesn't trust is that other people will be able to recognize this way of knowing. She struggles with it with her mother, she struggles with it with her husband, hiding her visions from him and thus separating the deepest part of herself from him.

In their journey she learns to take more risks and stop hiding this world from him and the community. Victor learns to broaden out from his "rationalist" position and accept the world of mysticism, which has its own kind of logic and is quite different from the scholarly approach he was used to.

Strangely enough Philip and I seem to be mirroring the initial great divide between Nadya and Victor. Philip doesn't really believe in past lives or clairvoyant peeks into the future. He explains it as a heightened sense of intuition. So we dance around Nadya's "seeing" as Victor and Nadya must have done many a time.

It's hard to come to terms when one has different premises of how the world works.

Philip: Quite so. And so maybe I am more like Victor. I do believe in what I would call intuition, that people can sense how things will unfold, but I don't think they can know. Intuition, for me, is an astute guess, at best.

And I do know that some folks experience their intuition in vivid inner images which they "see," especially super sensitive people. And, as far as things like reincarnation are concerned, I think it's just one of those things you believe in or don't, and I don't.

I do believe, however, that Nadya was wise, perceptive and had great natural intuitive talent. I believe she was super sensitive and such folks do experience vividly and with a strange multi-modal intensity. They smell colors. They hear images. I do believe she "saw" something, and whatever it was it was very important to her, a connection, a possible collaboration, a path into the future.

Marilyn: I am observing my own resistance to your framing of Nadya's "knowing." I feel that by accepting the framework acceptable to you, I am betraying Nadya, and maybe myself as well. This language of yours is not a fair representation of her. Victor and Nadya had that same struggle in their dance. She'd say to Victor "I got a vision in a meditation," rather than saying how it really came to her as a "knowing." She'd try to find ways to package her knowing so it would be acceptable to his worldview. There is a part of me reluctant to play that game anymore. Maybe my process and Nadya's have been similar. I've had to learn to come out of hiding and start saying it like it is.

Philip: I'm not saying you can't say it a certain way. I'm just saying how I make sense of it. I do believe she "saw" things he didn't.

She remembers translating her thoughts into his intellectual language. I suspect that she could play with his thinking in ways it's never been played with before. He is a scholar and a man who loves to learn. I bet she was fascinating to him, being all filled with forbidden thoughts as she was, and also being so solid. I think it was one of those soul-mate things where they needed whatever it was the other person had.

I do think it wasn't just that she was physically attractive (although he was careful to emphasize how important that was for him.) Even so, it took him ten years before he had an equivalent realization on his part about their relationship. And his obliviousness was hard on her. Part of that delay might be accounted for by the fact that Nadya, for many years, did most of the work in making the relationship run harmoniously and for many years kept much of the fact of that work and her "seeing" to herself.

Even so, even though she couldn't quite name it, she did see, or, as I would say, "intuit," in Victor, from the beginning, even when he was a young intellectual, that he was a man who could appreciate certain aspects of her character which she needed to live out. I suspect she could also see past his outer layers of intellectuality. The idea of many past and future lives, for me, was her perfect metaphor for how good the fit between them was going to be.

He just didn't have his breakthrough, or his vision – he called it a "revelation" – until they were on the edge of a crisis. Often we have to be pushed to these edges. Even then, for me, it was still natural phenomena.

I especially liked that he emphasized the importance of her physical presence in that revelatory moment in their living room. I do believe that partners potentiate each other. There are things you can say and reveal to one person that you can't to another. There was something in their connection, their palpable connection, which called forth wisdom.

Marilyn: The challenge for them and maybe any relationship is how you stay connected and still able to hold on to and express the most integral part of yourself, even when you fear that it will not be received by your partner. This is what Nadya and Victor have been working out together for the last 40 years. This is what they teach, how to be a mirror for the other… and how to take your partner to a place they can't go by themselves.

Philip: I suspect that, at some level, the intuitive connection was always there between them, but not appreciated, at least not equally by both. I think Victor probably, really, was always receptive to that connection with Nadya. Maybe he couldn't have named it at the time, but I suspect that even as she presented her mystical visions, there were things about those visions that were both threatening to his rationality but also fascinating. I had the sense he thought of himself as excessively rationalistic.

There were these two sides to their relationship. Head-over-heart encounters heart-over-head. What we see is that, at midlife, after a crisis-y time, they reconciled many of their differences and came to see the mirroring in their relationship.

In fact the moment of triumph for Victor came when he moved against conventionality and followed his heart and deliberately reversed his original priorities. He went to his son's game on Sabbath and was proud of it.

Victor: *And tough luck to God and all those people that said that wasn't the right thing to do. It was the right thing to do. All right? I'm proud that I made that decision. It's not just that it is the right decision. I'm proud that I made that decision.*

Marilyn: After 42 years of marriage they still struggle with that same delicate balance, how to respect their own rhythms and beliefs and yet stay "connected". So fitting that their current challenge is how they are going to function as a team. He, being 9 years older, is ready to slow down and she is bursting with energy to start new projects. Should Nadya just do stuff solo? Even this, Nadya says, must be decided jointly, as a team.

Philip: So, for this we have to be grateful to all the Rabbi couples and maybe give special acknowledgement to Victor and Nadya. There is a maturity and equality in their relationship and, at the same time, as they themselves have said, they are not in perfect harmony. The issues that challenged and fascinated them at the outset remain. They did not become more like each other but more resonant toward each other.

Perhaps that is one of my favorite lessons from this interview; this vision of what maturity can look like.

Marilyn: The irony for me is that in this chapter titled, Neshama Achat, (One Soul), we finally decide to step out of our Kol Achad, (One Voice). We finally decided that we needed two voices to express where we stand.

And I believe that this is a testimony to our relationship, how it has become stronger through our working together. We can trust each other more. We are not afraid to bring our different perspectives into the public forum.

And that takes us to the blue thread, which is what we do agree on. What we have come to understand is that the partners in a relationship must learn to appreciate how their relationship works. The partners must find the courage to express their differences with each other and do it with love. This takes time and generosity. Victor and Nadya have done this work. They appreciate how the pieces fit.

Nadya: *We are different people. And the beauty of our work together is that we've learned how to do that dance. We've learned how to dance where we really mirror one another, where we bring opposite attributes or experiences into the relationship. A lot of what we teach is about appreciating how what seems to be the opposite in your partner is what grounds you and completes you.*

Whatever it is that we're teaching together we're able to do that dance very, very fluidly, and we're very beautiful.

And they continue to do this work. As Victor said, *"It's not about a perfect relationship ... the excitement, the engagement, is in the perfecting."*

Chapter Seven
Being There

Rabbi Laura and Charles Kaplan

> *"So, this is what people mean when they say God is really there for you," the same way that Charles is really there for me, regardless of how I am performing. For me, that's completely transformative in how I understand my inner life, how to serve people at the synagogue, how I interpret everything spiritually."* -- Reb Laura

> *"She wanted to get up in the middle of the night to leave. I wouldn't let her. I said something like "I really think you could be the one for me." She thought it was a line and now 22 years later, obviously, it was not."* -- Charles

Again and again in these interviews we see how the shared story of love will revolve around a few key themes. With Charles and Laura one of the key themes is unconditional love. "No matter what happens, I will never leave. I am always there for you." What does this look like in real life?

Charles: The moment I knew? How embarrassing are we going to get? Well, I'll stay safe for the moment. Maybe if we get to know you better, we'll tell you the other story.

It was after we had been together for… It wasn't long. We'd been together day after day after day after day, every day, every night and we were sitting around in my living room with the fireplace on and just relaxing. And I said something like, "Well, I could really see this being a permanent thing," and you agreed. I don't remember exactly what the words were. Laura, you probably remember better than I do. That was sort of our statement to each other that this was really for real.

Laura: The story Charles is telling is about three weeks after we met.

Charles: The earlier one is the more embarrassing one. Oh God. Our first time we spent the night together. I was smitten.

Laura: [Laughter]

Charles: Laura was panicked. She wanted to get up in the middle of the night to leave. I wouldn't let her. I said something like "I really think you could be the one for me." She thought it was a line and now 22 years later, obviously, it was not.

Laura: When did I know? Well, I remember the very moment that I first saw him.

Charles: [Laughter] I know that story too.

Laura: Well, I guess it's a bit more context than Charles usually tells when we give the story. It was my first day working at the University of North Carolina at Charlotte and it was Charles' first day in a tenure track position there.

All the faculty went out to lunch and I was sitting with my colleagues and Charles came over to the table.

Later he said it was a deliberate move so he could be introduced to me. I looked at him and he was wearing a blue buttoned-down shirt.

Charles: Wow, what a memory.

Laura: And they said his name was Charles Kaplan, and they told him, "Congratulations on your tenure track position." And Charles made a joke. I don't remember the exact words but he managed to say in 3 or 4 words that he wasn't sure if it was so much of a blessing to now have his work scrutinized really, really closely and to have more responsibility. And I thought it was really funny. I thought, "Wow, he's cute. He's Jewish. I wonder if he's single."

Charles: Later, we met again at a wine and cheese party and there was dancing. And we spent the entire evening hanging out and dancing together and at one point I said to Laura, who I was clearly already interested in, "So your name is Dunham. Are you Irish?"

And her answer was, "Are you kidding?"

And then after the dancing, we went to an after party. At 2 o'clock in the morning, we went out for breakfast, and then we said good night.

Laura: And we made a date for two nights later, which is where Charles's embarrassing story took place. [Laughter]

Marilyn: Wow, so you knew really, really early.

Laura: But it really was about three weeks in when I came over to his house late one evening. We were sitting around in the living room. Maybe I had some work in my lap.

| | We just sort of looked around and said, "Wow, it might be possible to live like this."

So we're not the poster children for "develop a deep friendship, get to know each other first."

Philip: You know we've hardly met anybody who is.

Marilyn: All the people [we've interviewed so far] that have been together for 20 years and 30 years seemed to know right from the beginning. Or at least one of the two of them knows. The other one might take longer.

Philip: So how long ago was this?

Charles: 23 years. Wow.

Laura: Wow.

Philip: What were the sorts of challenges that came up for you?

Charles: The early days? Probably the first Yom Kippur that we spent together. First, some background. Judaism was Laura's natural habitat growing up and it's just always, always, always been part of her life. And for me I grew up in a very Reform, not very religious or spiritual, home. My mom lit Shabbas candles and we had Passover Seders. That was it.

So I worked on Yom Kippur because I was busy. That's just the way I lived. Laura was horrified.

Laura: I did spend a little time in Shul that day but I mostly stayed at home and cried my eyes out and I thought, "Oh, my God. Marriage was a mistake. This is so terrible." This was right after we got married.

And at the end of the day I called my mother and I told her what had happened.

	Then, a couple of days later, I heard the story in altered form back from my aunt.

At that point, I made a decision. I am an adult now. I will no longer share any details of my married relationship with my parents.

I don't know if we worked it out. We just moved on and the next year, you planned in advance and that was different.

So, I think our different observance levels was something of a challenge in the beginning. |
| Charles: | But only a little bit.

You know, as I spent more and more time with Laura and when we did more and more rituals and practices in our home, I got completely sucked in and absorbed in it. Now I can't even fathom living any other way than an observant life. |
| Laura: | Well, here's another fun challenge that we had early on. We were living together maybe a year and a half and we just did our own thing. We had very few conflicts over space or money. And then a week after the wedding, all of a sudden, we didn't like the way each other managed money and we each thought the other kept the space too messy.

Like all of sudden, we had signed the contract. We had sealed the deal and now there was a little program running in our heads about what married couples should argue about. But once we realized it was just about, "Oh, my God, we just got married!" then it went away as an issue. |
| Philip: | When you fought early on, what was that like? |
| Laura: | I don't remember a specific fight. Wait. |

Here is one, a fight with no substance whatsoever, but maybe it illustrates something in our relationship.

Charles: I have no idea what's coming.

Laura: Charles was talking on the phone with his dad and it was a really long conversation. And I really needed to talk to Charles. And every time I tried to say something or pass him a note, he kept saying "I'm on the phone. Shhh, I'm on the phone." Well, I got so angry with him that I took out my ironing board and my iron and I ironed all his shirts right in front of him. I laughed at myself later. I didn't know why I was doing what I was doing, but I was sort of saying, "But it's all about how much I love you!"

Marilyn: I get this clear image of the iron sizzling and the steam rising. I loved how you sublimated your anger. How about today? A current challenge?

Laura: We have two kids and they're 17 and 19. When they were small, we had a clear idea of what to do with them and had very few disagreements about raising them. But when they became teens, there were a number of situations that we fought about because neither of us had any idea what to do.

For example, is it okay for...oh, I can't believe I'm saying this ... Is it okay for our children to communicate to their friends that anybody can safely do drugs in this house because we will provide safety and support if anything goes wrong. That situation came up.

We certainly agreed that we would provide safety and support but neither of us had any idea what message to communicate to our kids, or how.

	We both felt at so much of a loss. It was impossible to have a calm and rational discussion because we didn't have any context for it.
Philip:	So what does happen between you when it's not possible to have a calm and rational discussion?
Laura:	There's like tension between us. Sometimes you can see it in ridiculous ways. Let's say, Charles comes downstairs first in the morning and then I come down second. And I don't say a cheery good morning and Charles says, "You didn't say good morning." And I say, "Whoa, you spoke in a grumpy way for our first conversation this morning."
	And, it might get resolved that morning or it might not. He might leave without saying goodbye. Then he'll come home in the evening and say, "Well, what was that all about?"
	So, when there's an underlying tension, it gets expressed in those very everyday kinds of ways.
Philip:	Some people stop everything when something like that comes up, but you guys just go on?
Laura:	Well, I think we, at least, have a basic understanding. If we're upset, we might not figure it out instantly. We usually give each other a couple of days.
	Then one person will say to the other, usually Charles saying to me, "What's going on with you?"
Charles:	My first thought if there's a bit of a shutdown or a lowering in Laura's mood, is, "Okay, what is she mad at me for?" But something may be going on with Laura that has little or nothing at all to do with me.

Marilyn: So can you give us a specific example?

Laura: He blocks those out.

Charles: I'll say that Laura has been struggling with some health concerns over the past couple of years and it had serious, serious impacts on her mood and even her capacity for rational thought. Neither of us knew what was going on until she finally got a diagnosis and started on a treatment plan. Before that, when Laura would be crabby and exhausted I would take that very personally.

Philip: Taking it personally. What does that mean?

Laura: I think "take it personally" means, "She does not love me anymore."

Philip: Really, you would still go there?

Charles: I always like to say that being a psychologist does not mean that you've cornered the market on mental health.

Laura: I think that sometimes we're so sensitive to each other's moods that we take a lot of things way too personally.

Charles: I would say that we're quite intensely sensitive to one another's moods.

Philip: Maybe that's the basic understanding you spoke about.

Marilyn: It's a blessing and a curse, a Jewish concept, maybe. Speaking of which, how would you say your Judaism shapes your relationship with each other. And also, how would you say that your relationship has influenced your Judaism?

Laura: Oh, well, I can definitely answer the second part of the question. Charles, do you want to answer the first part?

Charles: I would say that Judaism has given a joint focus for the cycles of our life. We look forward to all the different holidays, to all the different rituals. It certainly gives us a focus for raising our children. And it's given us opportunities to do things together. Like, we absolutely love *davening* (praying) together and we do it all the time at the Shul. I'm a musician. Laura is a very good singer. We sing well together and when we have the opportunity to do music together, it is quite nice. And of course, we end up arguing about it sometimes.

Laura: Yeah.

Charles: Because the only time we have to practice things is late at night when we're both crabby and we don't agree sometimes about how to organize a song. But we love it. It's a great opportunity. I wish we had even more joint projects.

Laura: Well, for my part our relationship definitely has given me a focus for my personal theology. But before I talk about my relationship with Charles, I want to say that my parents had a solid marriage but like a really terrible marriage.

They were together for the long haul. They shared many values but they fought all the time. They had much resentment that never ever got resolved, and which they confided to my brother and me. But it was still a household where love, unconditional love, was really, really strong.

I have no idea how I bumbled into meeting someone who really, really understands me. He's really comfortable with, capable of... really lives that idea of unconditional love and being there for you, and with you, even though our concepts of how we express it are not always the same.

And so I have come to experience God as love.

I think this came to me like deepest during the years that I was really sick, and maybe even during the time of pain. That was when I made this resolution that I was going to drag myself three blocks everyday to the local café, just about as far as I could walk at the time, and do some writing.

I remember one of the first few days that I was doing that. I'm sitting looking in the window and all of a sudden I realized, even though I feel so crappy all the time and some days it doesn't feel like life is worth living, there exists a few people in the world who really, really love me and accept me, and it has absolutely nothing to do with any qualities that I might have. It's nothing to do with my personality. It's nothing to do with anything. They're there for me simply because they made a commitment to love me; you know, my parents, one of my cats and Charles.

Philip: But not the other cat?

Laura: The other cat? No.

But just realizing that in that deepest moment, I thought, "So, this is what people mean when they say God is really there for you, the same way that Charles is really there for me, regardless of how I am performing, or of any of the things that I normally do when I'm healthy."

For me, that was completely transformative in how I understand my inner life, how to serve people at the synagogue, how I interpret everything spiritually.

That affected, and continues to affect, how I am as a counselor and a spiritual director. I had already learned in my studies what it means to adopt a listening posture with no distractions coming from your own self. But this really adds a dimension to the way I am with people and my sense of what it means to accept them with full attention and presence even though in day-to-day life at the synagogue there are times when they could drive me crazy.

So, it's important to be able to come from a place where it's okay with me that they are the way they are. That's what accepting them is about.

Philip: So you experienced it yourself and then you said, "Oh, that's what this is about." So then, that's what you try to do for other people.

Laura: It actually has really changed the way I deal with conflicts in the synagogue. I have a rooted understanding that we've chosen to come together as a community, that's the big container. Within that container, we're going to have some disagreements, conflicts.

They could be about policy or personality. Sometimes somebody on the board will come and say, "Oh, a really big thing happened," or "Oh...If this gets done, it will tear the synagogue apart." And because I'm able to think of the synagogue more as a loving family, I'm able to say, "You know, it's not really a big thing. There's no chance it will tear the synagogue apart. We are much too connected at the heart. Let's just think about how to be with it." And so, it really makes it much easier for me to be a non-anxious presence.

Marilyn: **That basic understanding again, yeah. Charles, what about this relationship has taken you to a place that maybe you couldn't have gone by yourself?**

Charles: Wow. I absolutely think that without this relationship I would not have become engaged in pursuing the spiritual path. Before I met Laura I spent time just trying to grasp, "What in the world are people talking about when they talk about spirituality and such things?"

And through just participating in our *Havarah* (Jewish spiritual community) in North Carolina, and moving to Or Shalom in Vancouver, meeting a lot of people who were on a spiritual path of some sort, I've had worlds open for me that I would never ever have imagined would open.

Because of that my family that I grew up in doesn't quite get me anymore. Like, "Where is he coming from?" It's hard.

They really don't get that when there's a holiday, you celebrate. I have to call my family and say, "Happy New Year." And they say, "Oh, yeah, it is Rosh Hashanah, isn't it?"

And my family *[of origin]* doesn't appreciate the fact that the focus of my life is not how much money you can make. It just is not. It's even less so now, as I do more things of a spiritual, helping, caring nature.

Marilyn: **And Laura, what would you say? Where has this relationship taken you?**

Laura: Well, I think that being married, or in a relationship of choice, for a really long time is an amazing thing. I really have to recognize everyday anew that Charles is a separate person from me. He thinks about things and experiences things differently.

I know that Charles said we're a lot alike. In a spectrum of human differences we are pretty close, but within that closeness, there are a lot of differences.

And it's nice to remember, every day, that what seems like natural and "of course" to me in my inner processes, are not necessarily that way for another person.

I know a lot of people use the metaphor of a relationship holding up a mirror so you can see yourself but that really happens. If I didn't have Charles asking, "Why do you think that?" or saying, "No, we're not going to do that!" I would not pause and say, "Whoa, how did I get there?" or "You mean the world isn't exactly like that?"

Obviously, I'm an extremely self-reflective person or I wouldn't have been a Philosophy professor and then a Spiritual Leader. But I

feel like Charles's approach to life and his being able to say, "Where are you coming from?" "What is going on with you?" has held up mirrors I would not have otherwise seen.

Philip: You started as a Philosophy professor, right? Was Judaism a parallel track?

Laura: *(to Charles)* Why are you laughing?

Charles: Because I'm stifling the urge to speak for you.

Philip: You want to answer her question? Go for it.

Charles: I said earlier that Judaism was Laura's natural habitat growing up. But also part of her habitat growing up was her deep need to question everything including her own perceptions. Being a philosopher was something that she came to at a pretty early age. Laura says that she pursued Philosophy in those days to get away from... How did you say it?

Laura:	Pursued Philosophy to get away from what was superficial in life.
Charles:	Right.
Laura:	And then pursued Religious Studies to get away from what was superficial in Philosophy. And then Psychology to get away from what's superficial in Religion.
Charles:	There. Thank you.
Laura:	It's the same set of existential questions and thinking and feeling processes. It was just that at different times in my life I encountered opportunities to study each of them.
Philip:	So many other couples struggle with how different they are from each other. They struggle with finding rules under which they can have difficult conversations. You guys seem so solid.
Charles:	Communication has always been pretty strong in our relationship. We've always been able to tell each other what we're thinking and feeling and work things out. Not to say that we haven't had times where that's been a real challenge, especially more recently. I think we have many, many, many years of knowing that we know how to talk to each other about challenging things that come up. Also that we have a base of similarities in our personalities, in our backgrounds, in our beings, that make it possible for us to do that.
Laura:	Oh, that's so beautifully said. Even though we have a set of rules about how to talk to one another and work things out, we did not get to them by sitting down and agreeing on them.

	I mean they are a combination of understanding things that we said to each other over the years about what we like and don't like to hear, or what makes us shut down and what makes us open up, and a combination of the things that we struggle within ourselves.
	Like one rule is no curse words when we're arguing with each other and trying to work something out because that shuts both of us down.
Charles:	Have we actually spoken about that?
Laura:	Yes.
Charles:	Oh, okay.
Laura:	Well, we didn't analyze it but I think at different times we both communicated to each other, "Don't say that."
	That reminds me of a story, I can't remember exactly the details. It's about something which was probably very small in the scheme of things. I don't even remember what it was. But all of a sudden, it was as if there was a rule broken. I thought, "Wow! People talk about those basic rules that people have in marriages. So much with us is just flow. We haven't explicitly articulated any of those rules and all of a sudden one of them has been broken.
	I found myself saying to Charles, "This is past my limit. If this continues, I don't want to be in this family." This was something big. Again, I don't remember what it was. It wasn't a big deal.
	I said it once to Charles and he said, "I totally get it. We're not going to do that anymore." And that was a revelation to me.

	Again, so much of our Relationship, the rules on how we act, have been by tacit agreement and haven't needed to be hashed out. This was like one of the first situations where I really thought, "Oh, wow, we do have all of these rules."
Philip:	It sounds like what was amazing was that you had to actually take a stand. What the stand was about wasn't so important.
Laura:	Yeah, I don't remember what it was about. The fact that this would happen 21 years into our marriage, all of a sudden, for the first time, I thought, "Wow!" And that I needed to be so passionate about the way I expressed it...
Marilyn:	And it sounds like, Charles, you got it right away. It didn't take you long.
Charles:	Absolutely positively. In other instances, it sometimes takes me a little while. I can be a little bit thick about getting Laura from time to time but I really do, I think, I work at it. I usually, sort of, come to it sooner rather than later.
Philip:	Yeah. Does she get you that quickly?
Laura:	I don't think so. What do you think?
Charles:	I agree. I think not.
Laura:	I think it's a pretty normal human thing, sometimes I don't get something about Charles until I have an experience myself. Then I say, "Oh my God, so that's what he's been talking about for the last 10 years." I could just give a simple example. You know, there are things in life that Charles feels insecure about, all right --
Charles:	Me?

Laura: Of course I don't get it because I don't think he should feel insecure about those things at all. I have very little patience when he says that there are things he needs from me because I don't understand why he should need those things.

But in the last few months since my mother died, and I lost a bit of this rug of unconditional love that I fly through life on, I myself have felt a deeper insecurity about a variety of things.

So then, a couple of days ago, when Charles said, "Well, I don't like your insecurity and I don't get where you're coming from," I did something in the moment that was really obnoxious.

I went upstairs to the bathroom and I got a mirror and I brought it down as if to say, "Charles, now you know how I feel when you say you are insecure."

But with a couple of days hindsight, I realized I should have flipped the mirror around and held it up to myself because now I understand where he's coming from when he's insecure and when I don't have any patience for it.

Marilyn: I love it. You communicate your feelings with objects, the ironing board story at the beginning and now, you with the mirror. Wonderful stories.

Philip: So you had to experience a mirror of the whole transaction before you understood his side of it.

Marilyn: **I just want to express our appreciation that you're allowing us into your private lives a little bit. How much of your lives do you allow to be public? I would guess that since Laura became a Rabbi that issue must come up often.**

Laura: It's funny. One of the congregants while thanking us for how we led the service, said, "If life at home is anything like it looks like out here, wow, you must have a great marriage!" We looked at each other and just laughed out loud because I think that was actually during a period where we were fighting a lot about something or other.

Charles: I was going to say, that as aware as we both are of how tightly connected we are and of how much we love each other, it always comes as a little bit of a surprise to me, less so now because we've been hearing this for many years, that it is immediately obvious when people meet us that we are deeply connected and love each other very much.

Laura: Yeah, one time we were at the Kallah (*Jewish Conference*) and it was the closing ceremony with about 600 people in some big tent and I was sitting about three quarters of the way towards the back with some people I've never met before. Charles was sitting on the stage in the middle playing guitar with Jack Gabriel. Charles is looking around the room smiling and the woman next to me who I've never met before said, "What's going on between you and that guitarist?"

Charles: So, it's a little bit embarrassing to say, but there are times when we're sitting in synagogue together when we just spontaneously reach out and hold hands while we're *davening*. I mean that may seem like a strange thing to do but we don't hide that. I'm sure people notice it and I think people in our congregation really love and appreciate the fact that we are so comfortable being affectionate with each other in public. That's definitely who we are.

Rabbi Laura Dunham Kaplan is the Rabbi at Or Shalom Synagogue, a Jewish Renewal Community in Vancouver BC **http://orshalom.ca**

Rabbi Laura and Charles
The Blue Thread in Their Love Story

God was Here and I, I did not know it.
Genesis *28:16*

Once again we were really captured by different aspects of the interview and couldn't quite agree on what the blue thread was. Here is how our conversation went.

Philip: What struck me was that quiet moment when their relationship crystallized. They were in the living room with the fireplace on and just relaxing and Charles said, *"Well, I could really see this being a permanent thing."* For me the quiet in that shining moment was not just "quiet" but a Quiet, not just the absence of noise, but a great tranquil space. It's underneath everything they do. That's how I see them. The blue thread should be "The Smooth Road." It seems so obvious.

Marilyn: Smooth Road?! I don't think that captures them at all. I noticed how often they shared stories about their disagreements. And how comfortable they were sharing their arguments and how these stories usually ended with lots of laughter and lots of forgiveness. There did not seem to be a shred of resentment between them. But Quiet? Smooth? No.

For me the blue thread would be something about unconditional love.

In my estimation their motto could be, "Love means never having to say I agree with everything you say."

What I learned from them is that unconditional love means you can disagree, you can disapprove, but you don't disconnect. You don't leave.

Even if you have to stand there ironing out every damn wrinkle in every damn shirt, you are not going away. You don't stop loving.

Rabbi Laura comes to understand how her relationship with God is like that, too. No matter how low functioning she gets when she's sick, she finally understands that God's not going away. God is there for her. God is unconditional love. And she has the same attitude towards her community. No matter how much they disagree, they are committed to each other. Disagreements will not break the community apart.

That's true for us, too, Philip. The more committed you and I are to our project and to each other, the more that we are comfortable disagreeing.

Philip: I couldn't agree more.

There is something good about our disagreements and it took us a long time to get there.

We get very serious with each other when we differ. When we speak of things we care about, we have strong feelings. And we have to speak our truth. For myself, I'm extraordinarily careful about finding very diplomatic ways to express my disagreements.

Marilyn: Why? What are you afraid of?

Philip: I'm afraid that if I'm not careful, if I push, the other person will simply dig in and shut down and I won't be heard. If I can't be heard, then I might have to leave or downgrade the relationship.

Marilyn: I didn't expect that. I expected you to say you were afraid the other person would leave.

Philip	Some folks are afraid of having to leave and some are afraid of being left. Either way, if you care about the relationship, it's a scary moment. So for me, how and when I speak up in the heat of an argument is always a strategic decision.
	Disagreements need to be done well. Charles and Laura do them well. There was something extraordinary about the way they remembered their disagreements. Their stories were more about how they handled them than about whatever the issues were. When I speak about the Quiet, this is what I mean. They have a safe way to contain all their struggles, a kind of spiritual crucible.
	I think we have that, too, a deep agreement that our conversation will be a discovery process. Under those terms, disagreements are interesting and welcome.
	We promise to really listen to each other.
Marilyn:	And not leave. Maybe that's commitment. There is something that solid about Charles and Laura, and I guess about us, too, at this point. There is no question of leaving. And that's what unconditional love is about, just being there.
	But when it comes to unconditional love, there is a fine line. It's like the fine print in the contract for unconditional love, the line you cannot cross, something about the rules of a relationship. Laura said that after 20 years she heard herself say to Charles, *"If you do that I will have to leave the relationship."* Even unconditional love has some conditions.
Philip:	That's very different than the understanding of unconditional love in my parents' crowd. I remember a joke they liked.
	A couple with a stormy marriage is asked if they'd ever thought of divorce. The answer was, "Divorce? Never!" "Murder? Often!"

                    My parents' marriage had a bit of that.

Marilyn: That's how Laura described her parents' marriage. Maybe Charles and Laura are the *Tikkun (the fixing)* of that marriage.

So after some joking and talking we did find a way to fit our differences together. The blue thread is both the Quiet and the noise, the container and the disagreements that it contains. Maybe that's another name for unconditional love. That safe container is what allows those arguments to cook up into something interesting.

One of the odd but common by-products of unconditional love is a certain pleasure in having arguments. You can laugh at yourself and your partner because it's safe and you know you're not going anywhere. But then we discussed what Laura meant by her realization about God and Love in the Coffee Shop. We decided to return to two voices. Some aspects of mature love are simply too complex to be captured only by one voice.

Marilyn: I liked how this couple came to understand God from the bottom up. They came to understand God through the way they loved each other.

Some people work more top-down, like Shefa. She says that God is her primary Love relationship and that Rachmiel, her love partner, receives the overflow. Shefa first "knew" God intimately, and then brought that intimacy to her love relationship with her partner. That's how it was for many of the other couples we talked to. They were Rabbis before they encountered their love partner.

For Laura it was different. She was with Charles for many years before she became a Rabbi. Twenty years into their marriage, she finally has an epiphany: God is Love.

God is always there for her through thick and thin offering total acceptance just as Charles has been. That's bottom up. Her love with Charles brought her to her epiphany about God.

Philip: Lovely. When I tried to think about top-down and bottom-up I thought maybe it was both, like Jacob's Ladder, with the angels going up and down. It's the sort of thing you can see after you've been through a few ups and downs yourself.

The bottom-up part means you learn about love by practicing it. Every time you and your partner meet a challenge, you commit yourself more deeply. I liked how Charles and Laura just hung in and hung in and eventually arrived at a place they would have never imagined.

And then there is the top-down part. Maybe for Charles and Laura, Love was calling them. We see the top in the distance and it draws us to it. As the poet Rilke said, "My eyes already touch the sunny hill going far ahead of the road I have begun. So we are grasped by what we cannot grasp."

After all, as everyone knows, the angels go up the ladder and they also come down. Committing opens us to Love and Love leads to Commitment. It's a cycle.

Marilyn: Which brings us back to God. Maybe God is always there for us but we don't always know it. Like Jacob when he awoke from the dream where he saw the angels going up and down the ladder said, *"God was here and I, I did not know it."*

Chapter Nine

All the Waters of the Flood Cannot Drown Love

**Rabbi Andrea Myers
and
Rabbi Lisa Grushcow**

> *Meeting Andrea was the best thing that happened in my life. Full stop. And it was also the best thing that happened to my rabbinate. By taking a different path, my learning and my feeling and my thinking, and just everything that shapes my rabbinate, became that much deeper by being more hard won and less obvious. - Rabbi Lisa*

> *It's a synergy when you have two people that love. Love is a good thing. But being able to complement each other and push each other, in good ways, is one of the gifts that I've gotten from you, Lisa, that I think I'm not willing to do without. - Rabbi Andrea*

Just when we thought we'd finished the book, Rabbi Andrea and Rabbi Lisa moved to Montreal and were enthusiastically embraced, not just by their own synagogue, but by the entire Jewish community. We waited six months to get our interview with them. We felt it was that important.

So much of their story is about love, faith and courage. In this respect they have much to teach the rest of us. They have been tested earlier in life and on more fundamental issues than most of us are ever tested. What we learn from them is that, when you meet your challenges with integrity, and love, it becomes contagious and influences the world around you.

Philip: **When a couple connects, there's some memory they have, a very specific memory. You may have the same one or separate ones.**

Lisa: No, it's the same one.

Andrea: Okay.

Lisa: Do you want me to start and then you will come in?

Andrea: Absolutely. She's the storyteller, I'm the writer.

Lisa: We had to go a long way even to meet. We met at an International Interfaith Conference in Bendorf, Germany. Andrea was in rabbinical school in New York and I am Canadian but was in graduate school in Oxford, England. We both ended up at this conference for our own separate reasons.

We had known about each other but we had never met.

Andrea: It was in the chapel. I had seen Lisa coming into the conference the night before. To say that the room was crowded would be a total understatement. It was packed to the gills with people from every part of the religious world wearing every possible religious garment you could imagine. It was like a comic book of superheroes. It was amazing

It was so packed that you couldn't get in the front door. So the Oxford English contingent had to come in through the window.

Lisa: We'd been driving from England, traveling for hours and hours and hours, and could finally get out of the car to stretch our legs and they had these windows...

Andrea: Windows that went straight to the ground.

Lisa: Very well-designed German windows.

Andrea: So I'm watching this little group of people come in through the window. It catches your eye.

	Where I come from, people coming through a window means something very different. I said, "Wow, that's actually quite interesting."
	So, I had noticed Lisa the night before and the next day I had the pleasure of sitting almost next to her in a Catholic service which had enough incense to make me want to die.
Lisa:	The idea is that you had to go to everybody else's religious services. It's a weeklong Jewish-Christian-Muslim conference.
Andrea:	As my lungs are beginning to close from the incense, I heard this, what I would call, this stained-glass voice, which is a very particular voice. It has almost no accent and it just fills the room with a certain timber that's unbelievable as though it says, "I should be working in radio."
	It was Lisa explaining. Lisa was sitting two seats away from me and there was somebody in between us and she was explaining her thesis to this poor woman who was very tired, and who'd had a long night.
Lisa:	And who had made the mistake of asking me about my dissertation.
Andrea:	A very specific topic for which there was one person in the world studying this topic of a woman falsely accused of adultery. It's one of the few things that you can get brought up on charges for without any witnesses. So it's a really fascinating rabbinic case and I happened to know that Lisa was one of the few people in the world working on this topic.
	So I'm listening in and that poor woman next to me is sort of slumped. It wasn't her. It was a very long night the night before for everybody.
	By the end of the Mass, I said to Lisa, "I think I know you," and she said, "I think I know you." And we began talking and we started laughing and having a conversation that would go on for 15 years.

But what was significant about that was that we both realized then, that we had a lot of work to do in our lives. So we met, we laughed, we shared for a week. And then we both went back to our different places in the world and didn't get together for a few months. I then flew to Oxford to see her. I knew right away.

Lisa: So we met in March and then in June

Andrea: And in June, we got together...

Lisa: And that was it.

Andrea: So really the clock started in June for us. And in terms of the crystallization moment for us, we were in Oxford shopping for food. I'm from America, it's a very different eating style than Canada, or anywhere else, but there was enough there that we could kind of work together. And I said...

Lisa: We were trying to figure out which milk to buy and you said...

Andrea: We should get the two percent. We've been getting that for years.

Lisa: Because it just felt like it had been forever. Right?

Andrea: Right. We were getting two percent, as if we have been buying milk together forever and ever. And it was just this realization: "This is the first time in my life I've ever felt that I could have a lifetime with someone and it would never be enough time."

Lisa: For me, I think there were a couple other moments. I'm thinking back when we were at Bendorf and Andrea said very nicely that we both had work to do. My work to do was that I thought I was straight. I was on track for the Jewish Theological Seminary which, at that time, didn't ordain gays and lesbians. I'd been accepted there and was deferring to study in Oxford.

	And so I meet this woman who just had this incredible pull for me, right? And so we're sitting together through this conference and we're talking and we're laughing and we're staying up late. And I realized: "If she's talking to somebody else, and there's no seat beside her, I'm feeling a little jealous." So I kind of have to work backwards and say, "Oh!"

I was keeping a journal at that time. So I'm writing in this notebook and as I'm sitting beside her, I'm shielding it with my hand as I'm writing. I'm figuring this out internally and I write, "I think I'm a little in love with A." And she's sitting there thinking, "Who's A?"

Marilyn: You're jealous of yourself.

Andrea: I'm like, what is this? I must know. So now I'm very curious.

Lisa: And the second moment I'm thinking of is when I got back to Oxford. There was a message on my answering machine. – How archaic is that? – And it's from Andrea. And I remember, vividly, the room that I was living in at that time, a beautiful room in a 16th Century manor house. I remember there's that little L-shape room and there's the window, the window seat and the little desk and the phone. I remember listening to that message and thinking, then, "I do not want to walk away from this. I don't know where this is going to go.

I don't know what's going to be. But my life will be poorer, I'll forever regret if I don't answer this call." So that was – that was that.

Yeah, it was pretty high drama in the beginning. Well, in some ways. And in other ways it wasn't.

Andrea: We were 23.

Lisa: I was 23, you were 26. We were babies.

Andrea: Back then you could be that age and have lived quite a bit. Nowadays it seems that everything gets put off and put off.

Lisa:	That's true. I mean, I'd been living on my own for six years, you'd been on your own almost a decade.
Andrea:	By the time we were where we were we had lived enough to know that it was the right thing.
	Looking back now at a 23 year old I could be thinking, "Twenty-three. Oh my God! Do you know what you're doing?"
Lisa:	Right.
Marilyn:	You mentioned high drama. What was that about?
Lisa	We were each on very different trajectories. So to come together was really an act against gravity.
Andrea:	Lisa's a very low drama person. Because when we have something that changes our trajectory it is very significant. That's worth noting. In general any change is drama, but Lisa had a very set path.
Lisa:	I was going to go to Jewish Theological Seminary and I couldn't go and be gay. So it was wrapped in all kinds of things. And it was very wrapped up in the question of, "Am I still going to be a rabbi?" That was something which had been part of my hopes and dreams for over a decade at that point. So, "Am I going to do this and if so how am I going to do it?"
	Meeting Andrea was the best thing that happened in my life. Full stop. And it was also the best thing that happened to my rabbinate. By taking a different path, my learning and my feeling and my thinking, and just everything that shapes my rabbinate, became that much deeper by being more hard won and less obvious. And also we've been not only each other's greatest fans but also we see things in each other that we can't always see in ourselves.

	So whether it's my congregational work or your writing and the organizational and creative work that you do, I think that we see things in each other and help each other grow in ways that we wouldn't ordinarily.
Philip:	Do you have anecdotes to support that observation?
Andrea:	Well, I wrote a book through Rutgers University Press in 2011 and that book only came to be because Lisa was writing this fantastic High Holiday sermon. So, it's about 4 o'clock in the morning of the day it was to be delivered. Now I'm always the stunt listener. That's the gift of having two clergy. You get to listen to each other's work and give helpful positive feedback. There was a moment in the sermon when the energy needed a little something. And she put in one of the stories that I had from living in Israel. Specifically this was a story about *Kapparah* and me liberating a chicken. One of the chickens got loose and I ran with it through the *shuk* (market) in Jerusalem trying to save this chicken, like an idiot and...
	(Note: Kapparah is a Yom Kippur ritual where a person swings a live chicken over one's head transferring one's sins to the chicken and then slaughters it.)
Lisa:	Wait. I have to interject and say I fell in love with her listening to her tell stories at this conference. That's the part that we didn't mention. Andrea is a master storyteller and she told these stories and she had me from go.
Andrea:	Well, that is very kind of you.
Lisa:	No, it's true, but she has these great stories and she was so generous to let me share this story and to let it be the, the end note, the missing piece, of my sermon.
Andrea:	So we put the chicken story in the sermon and there happened to be a literary agent in the congregation who heard it.

This woman says to Lisa, "I need to know the source of the story so that I can read more from that author." And Lisa, in that very encouraging way she has, said, "Actually, it's Andrea's; it's never been written before. She's actually very good and doesn't know how good she could be. You should sit with her. She could use some encouragement."

So I met with this agent, who was fantastic, and she signed me, sold the book, and I've been on a book tour for a year and a half. But that's only because Lisa believed in me enough to give me that kind of confidence and courage and to listen to my stories in a way that only she could, just as I had listened to hers.

You know, it's a synergy when you have two people that love. Love is a good thing. But being able to complement each other and push each other, in good ways, is one of the gifts that I've gotten from you that I think I'm not willing to do without.

Lisa: And absolutely likewise. When I met Andrea I had to decide if I was going to stay in Oxford for my third year and start on my doctorate or not. But Andrea said, "Listen, you should write this doctorate and take this opportunity. It's going to be a good thing in the long run." And it was. It bought me some wonderful time to figure things out in my life so I could go forward whole. Sometimes with the whole business of coming out and dealing with rejection and changing paths and all that you can end up pretty rough around the edges. So that extra year, and your help, bought me that time. I don't know that I would have done it if it weren't for your encouragement.

Another piece is that, when I started rabbinical school, having switched movements, I couldn't necessarily see myself in congregational work.

	It was you who, through your own experience and your own work, helped open my mind both to a different kind of Judaism and to what congregational work can be. And that's absolutely why I'm here. You know if you told me 15 years ago that I would be the rabbi of a congregation this size in the Reform Movement I would have probably laughed at you. All this is because of you.
Andrea:	Same thing. That I would be the wife of the Rabbi?!
	(Lots of Laughter)
Lisa:	We feel very, very blessed.
Andrea:	Yes.
Lisa:	In being with each other in this family that we've grown.
Andrea:	With two beautiful girls, who are everything for us; Ariella, who is nine, and Alice, who is three, and that's really where our energy goes when it's not here at the synagogue.
Marilyn:	**What would be an example, a story, about a challenge in the relationship, the growing edge?**
Lisa:	This move to Canada definitely has been a lot for us to take on. We were in New York for many, many years. Andrea is a New Yorker, born and bred. So to uproot our lives and our kids and our home and our connections and relationships and everything else and to come here has been a lot.
	Andrea has been a superstar in terms of being willing to follow this opportunity that I had, but we try to see it as an opportunity for all of us. But you know, that's God's challenges and growing pains. We knew it was big when we were taking it on. But I don't think you could know how big until six months in and you're still trying to get a Canadian credit card or whatever else it might be.

	But I think even more profoundly, it's been hard and a sacrifice on your part.
Andrea:	Well, I think it was hard for all of us. Take the house we moved into. Two weeks after we closed on the house there was a massive flood in Montreal so when we moved here, we had to live in a hotel for a few weeks.
Lisa:	With the two kids in one room.
Andrea:	Actually the kitchen was destroyed. They found asbestos in every wall. I had contractors peeing on the floor. I had to babysit people in a language I didn't speak. We had to have things rebuilt, fighting with insurance companies who didn't want to talk. It was a lot.
	As first time home owners – you have to understand, we were living in New York City with the pleasure of walking inside your apartment to a hole in the wall where everything went down – Now we were separating garbage into four different kinds of things...
Lisa:	And realizing the dirty diapers only got picked up once a week.
Andrea:	Having to cook in a basement on a broken basement stove and just being able to boil water for two little girls and Lisa for three months. Plus, I mean, it only got done in October and November and then the basement had water so we really didn't get done until almost the New Year in terms of being able to live. That was a real stress. My job was to make sure everyone had a smooth landing. Whether it was the kids or Lisa or whatever they needed, that was my challenge. And it was exacerbated by the physical space.
	The kids were real troopers with this. We were very lucky, we were just very lucky. You just go one day at a time. Our three year old had it best.

Every morning she'd wake up and say, "Is the kitchen done yet? Today the kitchen will be done." Like she would say it as a question and then a statement as if, she was going to say it and it would be done.

Marilyn: Baruch Sh'amar v'haya ha'olam. Blessed is the One Who Spoke and the world came into being.

Andrea: Right. A very Jewish thing. I think that was a lesson that the little one really taught us. So no matter how exasperated we were, the little ones helped us, especially because they knew that at some point it would change.

Lisa: I'm glad you brought up that piece about the house because, I'll speak for myself, part of what instigated the move was, you know, very much that model of *Lech Lecha (Genesis 12-1.* When God commands Abraham to go and leave everything behind.) It's important to stretch yourself and to take on new challenges.

Not to stay just because you're happy where you are but to think about where that journey goes. That's something that I thought about very much in terms of the stories that are shared, stories biblically and rabbinically.

But still it was a huge undertaking. Yet there was that balance of the importance of going and at the same time the confidence that we would find a way to make a new home and a new life. Just last night we were talking about a quote from the Song of Songs which actually was embossed on the seal for our wedding invitations which was *"Many waters cannot quench love."* And that's been a keystone for us, almost in jest, both because it was the topic of my dissertation which had to do with waters and bitter waters and thinking about what it does to relationships, but also with the flooding, with the notion that what matters, endures; if you remember what matters. It shapes our belief that we love each other and want to do right by each other, come what may.

Philip:	**So this is also about the relationship between your love for each other and your understanding and practice of Judaism?**
Lisa:	In terms of the Jewish piece, let's say for us it's very integrated.
Andrea:	It's a constant.
Lisa:	It's always been very integrated. The first thing you gave me was Franz Rosenzweig's "Star of Redemption", do you remember?
Andrea:	Yes, I do.
Lisa:	And we have Noah's Ark with all of the animals engraved on our wedding rings because that's always been…
Marilyn:	You definitely have a water theme going here.
Lisa:	We do somehow.
Andrea:	It was *parshat* Noah, when we got married. (The week when the story of Noah is read.) And it was the month after 9/11.
Philip:	In New York state?
Lisa:	It was before it was legal in New York State.
Andrea:	Ten years before it was legal.
Lisa:	But we had our religious wedding that we count really as our wedding back in October 2001, the one we're talking of now.
Andrea:	You have to understand, we got married before gay marriage was cool. Or interesting. It was just not done.
Marilyn:	No gay marriage at all, never mind Rabbi gay marriage, right?
Andrea:	Right. So here we have two Rabbis from different seminaries getting married. There were 120 people from all the different seminaries, people all showed up for this even if they didn't stay for the meal afterwards.
	It was in a synagogue in New York City and the outpouring from our colleagues is not something that we will ever forget.

	Because it was at a time, not only was gay marriage not discussed, New York had suffered this tremendous tragedy. A lot of people couldn't come because they couldn't get insurance for flights and all kinds of different reasons…you had family that weren't allowed to come from Canada.
Lisa:	Flights got cancelled.
Andrea:	But it was just understood that people would come. You know, there's no better way to fight terrorism than to have a big Gay Jewish wedding in New York City. That really drove us…
Lisa:	Because it was so soon after 9/11. What do we do? The city was a ghost town.
Andrea:	The city was closed down; no one would make eye contact. It was like Lamentations. If you read the Book of Lamentations, that was New York after 9/11. No one wanted to look at each other. Everyone was afraid. The person next to them was suddenly the stranger. And to be a stranger in New York was one of the worst feelings in the world.
Lisa:	Because there was a real coming together. But there was also in those few weeks after, I don't know the word for it…
Andrea:	A shadow time. There was a shadow that had fallen over New York and this was people's first *Simcha* (celebration) after that. A lot of people who had been in mourning for friends and colleagues they lost, this was the first time where they actually were able to celebrate, and I've never seen people celebrate like that. I mean, not because it was us necessarily, but because they needed this. Our friends needed this.
	And that was one of the reasons why I think our wedding invitation had that quote. You know, the floods don't destroy love; destruction doesn't destroy love.

When you talk about collective memory and when we talk about what makes something Jewish, it's not just about our story, it's about how we fit into collective memory. And life cycle events fit into that; people remember your life cycle events and the love that you have is a rock in the pond and you don't know how it's going to affect people.

And so 10 years later they say, "You should know that after 9/11 there was all this stuff going on for me but I came and it made me happy. Thank you for that." And you get that from time to time and you realize it's not just about you.

And I think that's the larger Jewish lesson for me, in terms of when we were married at that point. We lived this, it's impossible for us to separate it, you know. I can't see without my glasses, those are the lenses that I see the world through. Judaism is my lens for understanding life, liberty and the pursuit of happiness. That's how I understand life.

Lisa: The best metaphor you ever gave me, and this was something that helped me a lot, is the floor board metaphor. We talked about this because when I was trying to get my head around coming out and why does this matter and why does it need to shape things the way it does. Andrea said, "It's not like this is a room in your house that you can close the door and just not go to that room, it's like the floorboards, it's throughout the house, it's where we walk, it's how you live, it's just integrated." I think that Judaism is that, too, for us that it's not, you know, you get up and you go to the synagogue and you do your Jewish thing and then you go home and you do the rest of your life, it's integrated.

Philip: **But you know, at the same time, I imagine that you know much more about what it means to love now than you did 10 years ago.**

Andrea: I don't know about that. I think that at some level we teach each other how to love and especially with the children so I think that that's true but I think on some other level, thank God, for whatever reason, we were open to it and in many ways that we did not expect to be open.

You know, for where we were, in both of our lives, there should have been so many walls and so many red flags. Danger! Danger! Danger! That should have prevented all of this from happening in the first place.

Lisa: And there was nothing.

Andrea: And there was nothing. For whatever reason, it was always... You know how everyone says, "Just go to that happy place in your mind"? I didn't need to, I had Lisa. I had a real place that I could go to and not be afraid, a place where I was able to be myself. I didn't have to learn a new metaphor for love.

It's not that I came without problems but I could just be myself and that was new for me. It was very new for me. I come from the '80s in America under Ronald Reagan, you know, where everyone was a different person than they were pretending to be. I converted to Judaism. You know, you hear Lisa say, "15 years ago if someone would have said I was going to be a Rabbi..."

Well how much more so if someone had said to me 20 years ago, "Oh, PS, you're going to be a Rabbi", I would have laughed. I'm Sicilian and I'm German. I was raised Evangelical Christian. I was living on Long Island with the Irish and Italian in the middle and, you know, I went to Brandeis University and I didn't know it was Jewish.

I went to Brandeis because every mother wants a doctor and I graduated with a neuroscience degree because my mother said, "You can do whatever you want with your life but you're going to graduate with this major because that's how it's going to be and you're going to do it." So I did what I was told and then I lived in Israel for a few years.

Philip: **But nonetheless there are realizations. Take the realization that Lisa was a real person you could go to for real love. How did that change the way you understood your spirituality?**

Andrea: Well, we're Mitnags.

Philip: I don't know that word.

Andrea: So let me explain...

Lisa: We're Mitnags, Mitnagdim. We're not – our spirituality is not Hasidic or neo-Hasidic.

Andrea: What you see is what you get.

Lisa: For us, our spirituality is not connected to study. It's connected to practice. We're not Kabbalists. We're not mystics. It's not to say there's not the other spiritual piece.

But I would say that one of the things that I've learned over the years, and really learned from you, Andrea, is that you don't take love for granted, you don't take our relationship for granted, and you don't take another person for granted. All that is something that is renewed every single day, something that needs tending and attention every single day.

And that's, in a sense, a Mitnag's approach, the notion that you're known by your actions. I can believe whatever I want and I can say whatever I want but I can only show you that I love you. To tell you that I love you does nothing. It's "How do I live and how do I make time and how do we not take each other for granted."

Andrea: You know, I feel like on some level God is with us all the time and this is it. I'm not a shepherd, I'm a sherpa. (In Tibet, a person who carries stuff for others who want to climb the mountain). I'm not going to pretend I know more than anybody else.

There's no great magic out there. This is what we've got. I'm not going to pretend to guide people around with my big shepherd's hook but I'll carry the load up the mountain. I'll help people. I'll walk with them.

Our vision isn't that, as spiritual leaders we know more, that we're more enlightened. We're not coming down from on high to give someone the truth with the capital "T." We're very much in this world. We struggle just like our congregants do.

And what we can share is certainly -- I can only speak for myself here -- is how to build a Jewish identity from the ground up, how to live your life in an integrated way, with joy and with happiness, and to understand that God has a sense of humor, and love, and that you can trust that, no matter how bad it gets. That form of spirituality isn't necessarily expressed in the more common rubric of Jewish spirituality, but for us, it's a legitimate one.

Philip: You used an interesting metaphor, "carrying the load," "being a Sherpa." What would be a specific example of that in your everyday life with Lisa?

Andrea: We were both blessed with parents that have been together really a long time, and lived through a lot of stuff, and they never left each other and that helped me understand "You don't give up." So I don't give up on people. I don't. That's how I roll. I will follow to the bitter end. I'll do a Thelma and Louise if need be. And we're going off that cliff and that's going to be that. Bring it on.

	But I think that, you know, one of the carry-the-load things that we talk about with our relationship is "portfolios." We divide up the jobs that we have in our relationship by portfolio. So Lisa is Religion and Education portfolio. I am Homeland Security and Entertainment.
Lisa:	I do Finance.
Andrea:	Right. I'm Arts and Leisure.
Lisa:	Right. But it works. It works for us, right?
	So when Andrea was asking before about the interview and will we be able to see it before it's published, that's Homeland Security.
Andrea:	And Lisa will answer the Mitnag question because that's Religion and Education. We just have a natural Go-To that we created from nothing.
Lisa:	Which, I think, actually is an advantage in same-sex relationships because there isn't the default. You know, the guy changes the light bulb and the woman takes care of the kids. We don't have that default. So what we have the ability to do is play to our own strengths, which fortunately are complementary. Right? You cook, I clean. You could probably clean better than I could cook, in terms of cleaning but it works the way it works.
Marilyn:	It's a meritocracy
Lisa:	We found our rhythm with that very early on. It's true with emotional things as well as practical things.
	And that, when you talked about building from the ground up, it's the groundedness, the awareness, that whatever you're doing, you're doing it for good a reason. Right?

So even though both our portfolios have that fun stuff and the less fun stuff, it's like that story that's trite but true, about the person who's building something and someone asks, "What are you doing?" and the first person says, "I'm making a brick", and the next person says, "I'm making a wall," and the next person says, "I'm building this beautiful cathedral to praise God."

So when you take out the garbage or vacuum the house you could be doing any of those things.

It can be, "Ugh, I've got to do this. Why am I the one who's doing this?" or it can be, "I'm doing this as part of this bigger project, this relationship, this family, this home that we're trying to build." That's holiness.

Andrea:	I'm always shocked at how much *how much* you encourage me.
	For instance, I'm on the board of this wonderful organization, Keshet, *(meaning "rainbow")* which is an organization for LGBTQ Jews and there was a board meeting in San Francisco a few months ago and I was very hesitant about going. It was the first time I was travelling. My papers weren't exactly in order. I was terrified to get on that plane and you were so encouraging. You gave me the strength to do that. I didn't think I had it. Just to get out that door! You really pushed me in a good way. Genesis refers to *Ezer Kenegdo*, someone who helps in a way that doesn't just enable.
Lisa:	Right. The translation usually is, "Help-meet" but it's literally "a help against..."
Marilyn:	This is a reference to the creation of Eve.

Lisa:	That's right. Andrea is my help-meet, the person whom I can trust. In congregational life, they'll always be someone to tell you that what you do is great. And they'll always be someone to tell you what you could do is terrible. You need your own really finely calibrated sense of your own self and right and wrong and accomplishment.
	And you also need someone who could always tell you the truth, whether it's an easy truth or a hard truth. And, Andrea, you do that for me.
Andrea:	Well it's a team job. This rabbi gig here is not a one person job. It's like being on a baseball team and you are the pitcher. But it's like the Yankees, in that there are no names on the back of the jerseys. You see the team and the number, but you don't know really who's doing what. We are very happy to serve. It's a privilege to serve, but there's a lot that goes on behind the scenes that no one has any idea.
Lisa:	It's true.
Marilyn:	**We found that in every Rabbi couple, the two of them are making the rabbinate work. In your case, you're both Rabbis so how does that work? For example, Andrea, how much of your rabbinic experience do you bring to this situation?**
Andrea:	Every bit of it. You need every tool to get through it. Lisa knew me as a congregational Rabbi for five years and also, I did administration in my seminary as soon as I graduated.
Lisa:	I was in full Rebbetzin mode for at least five years...
Andrea:	I took care of everything for us while she was in school. And you know, the moment that that changed is when I was pregnant with our first daughter and we made the decision that we were going to raise our own kids.

	So we decided we wouldn't have a full-time nanny and we were going to do this the way we were raised. And that's why I left being a congregational Rabbi.
	But we're different Rabbis in general. Lisa's fantastic at big congregations. I like the little stuff, where the congregations are small, where I set up the chairs, some light plumbing, things like that.
Lisa:	She caught the bats at the last congregation...
Andrea:	I caught the bats.
Lisa:	Sha - BAT Shalom!
Andrea:	I had the whole thing. It was really quite funny.
Lisa:	But if I can jump in, what you've done really well, Andrea, has crafted what it means to be a Rabbi *connected* to a congregation where you're not the Rabbi *of* the congregation right?
	And so, Andrea teaches our introduction to Judaism classes here. She's the one who makes those real connections for our students coming in. Conversion students, people who are marrying somebody Jewish. She's a master, master teacher and at the same time, if I can say this, you're going and you're bringing a Shabbat dinner to one of our congregants who's older and who's sick.
	And you do this organizational work, and you serve on this national board and you're an author and you've written for the Huffington Post, and your book, and she's going to Gay-Straight Alliance next week to speak to them and so on and so forth.
Andrea:	I'm a busy unemployed person.
Lisa:	But I think you really are redefining what it means to be both – I mean, we're both Rabbi and Rebbetzin and so there are times where each wears one hat more than the other, but we're integrated, and we're making it work. And there aren't so many models out there.

Andrea:	I'm so glad we're gay. It really helps to be gay, because they don't know what to expect. So we tell them.
Lisa:	It's true.
Andrea:	And we'll create a new Heaven and a new Earth. So we're going to make a totally new model without the gender binary, without the expectations. You have two seconds to make that impression.

And if you can make someone smile, if you can make them laugh, you can give them that moment of joy. You take them away from, "Who's in the suit? Who's got the pants?" You gotta take people out of their challenge zone and put them into a comfort zone. Help them understand that, those old models, they don't have to apply. |
Lisa:	Right. Because I think a lot of women who are married to men who are Rabbis, deal with an expectation of a conventional Rebbetzin role. I think a lot of women who are Rabbis and married to men struggle a lot with how they are seen, and what's the transference in terms of gender and sexuality.
Andrea:	How they're dressed.
Lisa:	Yeah, what they are wearing. But, because we are working with a different set of assumptions, we can make up the rules a little bit more and unbalance things just enough that we can go ahead and do the work that needs to be done without it being all about "What's the rabbi wearing or what's the rabbi's wife doing". It gives a certain freedom to do the work that needs doing, in our own way, to serve the people we serve.
Andrea:	From day one this congregation has welcomed us with open arms.
Lisa:	Including our rabbinic colleagues in the city.

Andrea:	So it's a learning process. But we don't pretend to know any more than what we know that day. I think that if there's one thing you can say about this, that's it.
Lisa:	Recently we had a number of Catholic seminarians who visited for a service. And I remember thinking to myself that I have great respect for what they're doing and how they're doing it, but I can't imagine doing this work not embedded in family and in relationship.
	Not that you need to be married to be a Rabbi or to have kids to be a Rabbi, because God knows there are plenty of our colleagues who are neither, and doing magnificent, magnificent work, but for me, that groundedness in the day-to-day family, gives me more compassion, it give me more humility. It gives me more connection.
	For instance, the first time during holidays here, doing the family service, you were sick and couldn't be there.
Andrea:	I was really sick.
Lisa:	We had a new babysitter, who was fabulous, but to whom our very attached three-year-old was not yet attached. So there I am leading the service and my three-year old is holding on to my leg, or sitting in the seat on the bimah *(the Rabbi's podium)* and the people in the congregation who have been there with their kids, can look and say, "Okay this is where I can find a place and I don't need to worry if my kid does something out of sorts. This is a place where everybody can come in." I think that's something we really try and model.
	I don't know if I have a better example. That was the first that came to mind.
Andrea:	Well what do you want an example of?
Lisa:	An example of how being in family or relationship makes me a better person. No, you do, and you make me a better Rabbi.

Andrea: Well, two Rabbis are better than one.

Lisa: For sure.

Andrea: I mean, for the most part. One of the things that Lisa and I do, which I love, is the two-for-one. We are a really good team. We can make it look seamless. The hand-off which no one will see is like a magic trick.

She has something to prepare and I know she needs a little piece of something, or I need a piece of something, which is exceedingly more likely, and it just gets done.

Lisa: For one thing, because you're not as formally connected to the congregation, you can reach people who have issues with institutional Judaism or congregational Judaism.

People who wouldn't necessarily be able to walk through the door in the first place, you can help them find a home here.

Andrea: Right. I mean, I think our Seder's the best example of this. So for our second night's Seder, one of the things that I had been doing in New York for many years was inviting all of my introductory students to Seder in our house. So people who have not had a Seder before, or who may feel on the margin, those are the people that we want in our house. We really wanted to make that statement, "Come and eat at our table."

So we had a Seder in our house with 36 people, the most eclectic, wonderful group of folks. I cooked everything and I served everything. I made a hundred matzo balls plus. I had the whole thing going. And you were able to lead the Seder so it was a real hand-off.

Lisa: It's not just that the congregation benefits from our being a family, it's also that our family benefits. I love that our kids grow up seeing all those different people coming into our home and being welcomed at our table.

	Our kids grow up seeing that practice, in some ways very traditional and in some ways very not. I think it's a great gift to be part of a community in that way.
	Our kids were beloved in our congregation in New York and they're getting to be known and at home here. It's a huge gift.
Andrea:	There was a moment for me. Our daughter, Ariella, loves to help out as an usher. She loves giving out books and telling
	So the head usher made her her own little name tag that says usher-in-training. And she put this on her door. It meant something to her. She wouldn't let anyone touch it because it really made her feel like a part of this congregation and she wants to take her place. For me that was the moment when I knew it was going to be okay.
Marilyn:	**Is there a line for you between your public life and your private life?**
Andrea:	We don't talk about our kids.
Lisa:	In any way that would ever be kind of embarrassing to them.
Andrea:	We don't tell cutesy stories about our kids on the potty. We'll tell benign stories but we protect our kids. That's a big line for us.
Lisa:	I think we're respectful of each other's privacy and also of the privacy of our congregants. So if something is told to you in confidence you keep that confidence.
Andrea:	I don't tell Lisa everything everyone tells me.
Lisa:	No, and likewise. Because people need to be able to trust us and to know that we have those boundaries. We're not here to be buddies. We're here to be rabbis and to do this holy work together of building community.

	That requires some time for peace and quiet and reflection. So I'm pretty protective of the time that I do have with my family and with my home because that's my covenant with them, and that's my promise to them,
	And if I don't take that seriously, how can my congregants expect me to take their lives and their commitments seriously?
	And so that's an important piece. So we'll invite people into our homes for specific occasions, and we'll do so warmly, and whole heartedly and...
Andrea:	But there's a line.
Lisa:	So if I'm putting my kids to bed, I'm not picking up my phone.
Andrea:	That's it. No, we don't do that.
Lisa:	And our kids need to know that our home is their home first and foremost. So we try to be pretty thoughtful, I would say.
Andrea:	We're very human people. We're not fake, and the best part about this job, at least for me, is that I don't have to be a different person. It's not like, from 9:00 to 5:00 I'll have to be a different person, and then I talk on a phone and pretend to be somebody different. This is it for me. And you are the same person now as I remember this morning.
Lisa:	Rushing the kids out.
Andrea:	Rushing the kids out and everything else, you know, consistency of personality and type takes a lot of time, a lot of crafting. It's something you grow into, but it's a goal, and it's what we're going for here.
Lisa:	That's really interesting because, you know, coming here, for me, I'm here to be a Rabbi. And there's a certain amount of buzz: Oh! The woman Rabbi! Or the gay Rabbi!
Andrea:	It's not an issue for her.

Lisa:	And it's really an art form to answer those questions in a way that shows that I'm totally comfortable in my own skin and we have nothing to be ashamed of and everything to be proud of in the life that we built. At the same time it's not the point, and it is private, right? And so one of the newspapers was asking questions about how our kids were conceived and that's nobody's business.
Andrea:	That's right.
Lisa:	That's our family.
Andrea:	So we don't ask you and we don't want to know. We really, really don't care.
Lisa:	Yes. And so on the one hand modeling, you know, really being proud of, and human in, one's life, and on the other hand, it's not about us. It's not about me in that sense, and that's really important. Because I think that in the rabbi business, ego can be a real distraction, along with personality and charisma and all of those things. You need to be the kind of person people want to connect with and listen to and learn from. But the moment that you think that it's all about you is the moment that you start making really awful mistakes, ethical mistakes and relationship mistakes.
Andrea:	That's the love part.
Lisa:	Yeah, this is about integrity. This work is nothing if you don't have integrity. And when you start losing those boundaries between public and private and taking advantage of people who don't have those boundaries so firm, for whatever reason, that's a real danger zone.
	That's something that we're both so strict about. You just don't take advantage of people.
	You don't mix up public and private. I know who I come home to and where my heart is. I give body and soul to my work and it's not just work. It's never just a job.

And at the same time I know that part of doing that right means understanding that it cannot be the entirety of who I am. That I go home and wash the dishes and then take out the garbage. And much more important than all of that, I need to show these three people in my family that they are my be-all and end-all.

And so that keeps you grounded and it keeps you whole but it also keeps you from making mistakes, I think, either just from thinking too much of yourself or thinking too little of yourself, or for all of those slippery slopes when it comes to relationships.

Andrea: I hope this helps.

Philip: That was great. That's great.

Andrea: We eat cheese and play Scrabble for fun. We still laugh after all these years. It's very hard to make me laugh. I come from very wonderful, funny people and...

I laugh but, you know, you still make me laugh and I love that because I never see it coming because for me humor is a reaction to the unexpected so it's like how can this person that I've been with for almost a decade and a half right now have shown me something different and yet you do. A Fine Mind. This woman has a fine mind and I love it. And she looks awesome in a business suit.

Marilyn: You've talked about how she still surprises you. Has this relationship brought out a part of you that surprises you? What still surprises you after all this time?

Lisa: I think one of the biggest and best surprises is when Andrea showed me that the world is a big place. I grew up as a more traditional Jew. But now I see that how we practice is important to our Judaism, but that it's a means to an end rather than an end itself.

	For me, as someone who by personality and training can tend towards looking for the rules, the black and white, the do-this and don't-do-that, you have shown me that the world is not even different shades of grey, it is much more colorful.
Andrea:	It's a big tasty place.
Lisa:	A beautiful tasty place. I'm thinking of that scene in The Bird Cage, with the Nathan Lane character, and he manages to put himself in a very somber business suit.
	But he has these bright pink socks, and he says, "One wants a hint of color." And you have constantly surprised me by showing me the beauty of that hint of color. That's what I talked about when we talked about becoming a better Rabbi and a better person. Because it gives me more compassion, and more appreciation, and more awe and wonder. And I'm very grateful for that.
Andrea:	Also that you eat blue cheese now and sushi.
Lisa:	All kinds of things I never ate before I've never...
Marilyn:	You get the color in the cheese now too.
Andrea:	She's still kosher, but when I met you, you had been vegetarian for 13 years, and I was like, "I don't know if I can do this."
Lisa:	You were very patient.
Marilyn:	**Andrea, how would you answer that question about what surprised you?**
Andrea:	I'm exceedingly shy to the point of painfully so. Put me on a bimah *(podium)* or put me in front of people and I'm able to light up.
	But the truth, left to my own devices, I am exceedingly hermit-like, quiet... You made me social and that shocks me. That I am able to communicate my stories and communicate as well as I do is only thanks to you.

Whether it's art -- because I do a little bit of art and music and things like that -- that I'm able to communicate as well as I do, is thanks to Lisa, no doubt. I was raised to keep my mouth shut and my head down. I was raised in a very traditional Christian home. They would never identify as such. They would just say they were "American." But I know what they are now. They are Republicans, people who are very, very traditional, who never talked about sex or politics or religion. I didn't understand what it meant that my grandmother worked for Nixon or any of this stuff. I didn't understand.

So when I came out I wasn't met with, you know, any happiness. We both had our difficult time, but for me, for my family, I had four gay cousins and I didn't know it. I wasn't told. So it was, you know...

My mother met Lisa – and you should think Bea Arthur when you think of my mother – and she said, "Stop now. You're good. This is as good as you're ever going to get." She held my hand and she looked in my eye – and she never does this – "Stop now."

And the joke that we tell, but it's absolutely true, is that the doctorate helped me because Lisa had one and my mother wanted me to marry a doctor. So she can tell her friends, "Oh, my daughter married a doctor."

Lisa: So for the record, for the distribution of labor in the house, I take care of vomit, she takes care of blood. Because I could never be a doctor.

But I don't think you ever thought you would be married with kids.

Andrea: No, I thought I was going to have an '80s life, you know because I was told "If you're gay, you're going to be alone."

Lisa: Right. Because I always imagined that I'd get married and have kids.

Andrea:	We'd already been religiously married in 2001 and we were already married civilly.
Lisa:	It wasn't a marriage. It was a domestic partnership.
Andrea:	Now, it's two or three years later. I'm pregnant. She's reading the New York Times. It's Sunday morning and I'm sitting down and I'm pregnant, I'm angry, I can't eat enough food. "Another piece of toast." And she looks at me and says, "Marriage has become legal in Canada. You cannot give birth out of wedlock." I was like, "You have got to be kidding. What are you expecting me to do?"
Lisa:	We drove to Kingston.
Andrea:	No, I drove us to Kingston, still angry the whole time, to get married by a 15-year-old in cut-off short shorts who did it wrong and it took three years for them to get the paperwork right because it was right after it became legal. But it meant something to you, and that was enough for me. So we did it.
Philip:	**For you, what story in the bible is a good metaphor for a love relationship? For me, for instance, it's the story of Jacob wrestling with the angel.**
Andrea:	I would say for me it's the Jacob dream story. In the dream there are angels going up and down on the ladder but at the end of it, he finally understands and says, "God was in this place and I, I did not know it." He calls the place Beth El, the House of God, not "the place of God," which is fascinating. He recognizes that there was stuff he didn't know, that God was there. That, for me, is what a loving relationship is like. I wouldn't believe it if I hadn't seen it with my own eyes.
Lisa:	For me it would be when God says, to Adam just before he creates Eve. "Let me make you a help-meet," like I was saying earlier. Literally, it means "a helper against" or "across from."

It is a notion that through both agreement and expansion that we become our best selves.

But also, while we're talking biblical metaphor, I remember when we were in Albany when there was all the debate about marriage, and marriage equality and there were these very fundamentalist religious groups protesting against it. And it was the whole "Adam and Eve, not Adam and Steve" argument. But if you look at Biblical stories, sure, it's Adam and Eve. But it's Jacob and Rachel, and Leah and Bilhah and Zilpah; and it's Abraham and Sarah and Hagar.

What we think of now as traditional monogamous heterosexual marriage, we don't find that in the Torah.

So the point is, just like with metaphors for God, so also with models of marriage, there are so many, precisely to keep it from being stultified, to keep it from being written in stone that "This is what a marriage looks like." Because then, you do take it for granted. And then you assume either you fit or you don't fit and that's the end of the story.

I think my metaphors are not from the stories of relationships in the Torah, but from things beyond. I go back to what I said at the beginning of our conversation. It's like God renewing every day the work of creation. You've got to renew your relationship every day.

Rabbi Lisa Grushcow is the senior Rabbi at Temple Emanu-El-Beth Sholom in Montreal, Quebec.
http://www.templemontreal.ca/

Rabbi Andrea Myers is the author of **"The Choosing: A Rabbi's Journey from Silent Nights to High Holy Days"** *(Rutgers University Press, April 2011).*

Rabbi Lisa and Rabbi Andrea

The Blue Thread in their Love Story

God said to Abram, "Leave your country, your people and your father's household and go to the land I will show you." Genesis 12:1

It's the kind of moment that we both hope for and fear. Young Abram has a family, a community and a career and he gets a calling. He is told to leave the world he knows and is comfortable in. He is not told what he will find. First go; then see. Yes, just give up everything. Details to follow.

Committing to a life with someone is a kind of spiritual transformation and this is how spiritual transformations work. You don't know what you are getting into; you don't know where the road will lead; it's a leap of faith and all you know is that you have to take it.

Taking the leap is a powerful exercise. One of the greatest rewards of this is greatly enhanced faith, courage, and integrity. And this, in turn, changes your life, your partner's life and all the other lives you touch.

This leap is the blue thread in Lisa and Andrea's tale.

Lisa: *That model of Lech Lecha (Genesis 12-1. When G-d commands Abraham to go and leave everything behind.) It's important to stretch yourself and to take on new challenges. Not to stay just because you're happy where you are but to think about where that journey goes.*

This is their blue thread.

Lisa still remembers the moment vividly, down to the lighting in the room, when she received "the call," literally and figuratively.

She looked at the telephone answering machine and heard a voice in her head saying, *"I do not want to walk away from this. I don't know where this is going to go. ... But my life will be poorer, I'll forever regret, if I don't answer this call."*

This was a great test, a step into the unknown. She really didn't know how things were going to unfold. Her initial fear was that she would have to choose between her love for Andrea, and her wish to become a Rabbi. It turned out not to be the case but at that moment all she knew was that she was going to have to leave the life she planned in order to live the life that was waiting for her.

There was always this sense of destiny and they both shared it. After their first conversation at an academic conference Andrea remembered thinking, *"This is the first time in my life I've ever felt that I could have a lifetime with someone and it would never be enough time."*

If you are hardworking and gifted, the chance to co-create with someone else, equally gifted, who understands your vision, whom you can trust, who has a different but compatible vision – all that has an attraction that is almost tangible.

Lisa and Andrea both saw how they could empower each other and they saw it in fairly subtle terms. There is a fine line here. There is a big difference between simply admiring another's potential and actually having a critical and intelligent view of it. The great gift is to have a partner, who is critical and credible, and also positive and encouraging. One gets a sense that this is something they learned through their time together.

Lisa: *You need your own really finely calibrated sense of your own self and right and wrong and accomplishment. And you also need someone who could always tell you the truth, whether it's an easy truth or a hard truth. And, Andrea, you do that for me.*

Andrea: *I think that at some level we teach each other how to love and ... thank God, for whatever reason, we were open to it ... [With] Lisa I had a real place that I could go to and not be afraid, a place where I was able to be myself. I didn't have to learn a new metaphor for love.*

They inspire each other to reach each other's highest potential. It is like those Biblical moments where God, or an Angel, leads someone to go beyond their old life, to take the risk. Just go. Take that step. You'll see. You'll be glad you did.

The confidence and optimism, call it "faith," was an important part of this blue thread but only if it was faith-in-action. They emphasized that they were "*mitnagdim,*" which meant that their actions count more than their words and their walk is the measure of their talk. They are very "can-do." Troubles for them are just "*God's challenges and growing pains.*"

This kind of faith is contagious. They inspire each other, as well as people close to them. The metaphor they used in the interview was "throwing a rock in the pond," and how waves would radiate outward.

They've stayed true to a vision and a calling despite their fears that it would cost them everything they wanted and in the end, they got everything they wanted.

Lisa: *It's like that story ... about the person who's building something and someone asks, "What are you doing?" and the first person says, "I'm making a brick," and the next person says, "I'm making a wall," and the next person says, "I'm building this beautiful cathedral to praise God." So when you take out the garbage or vacuum the house... It can be, "...Why am I the one who's doing this?" or it can be, "I'm doing this as part of this bigger project, this relationship, this family, this home that we're trying to build." That's holiness.*

If your vision is big enough and you stay committed to it, love will make everything possible.

Afterword
So, Under the Bed,
What Did We Learn?

In most of the essays, we've spoken in one voice. But we are two people with very different sensibilities.

We decided to answer this question in our separate voices.

So, Under the Bed, What Did I Learn?

By
Philip Alan Belove

Now I have to take some of the same risks the folks in these interviews took when they shared their personal lives with us. Eeek. I don't know if I can explain how safe it was for me to be speaking in the "we" voice. I have to stop being that man behind the curtain and be me, Philip Belove, the guy who, despite being a psychologist, has a few things to learn about love.

Well, maybe that will never change. I do enjoy being that kid under the bed. I really want to learn more about what happens when admirable people love each other. (See how, in that previous paragraph, I transitioned from calling myself a "man," to calling myself a "guy," to calling myself a "kid"? It's vulnerability time.)

First, let me get this one piece out of the way. I'll be brief. The project greatly enriched my professional thinking. It fleshed out many ideas I'd acquired in school and training and supervision. Perhaps I should write a paper about it. Now let's look at the more personal stuff.

I started this project with Marilyn looking for fresh dreams about what love could be. What I learned did calm me down in many ways. It reassured me that I was doing okay about many things. But it also challenged me. It made me want more and it showed me where I could do better. All in all, it reshaped how I show up in relationships,

These interviews and stories went into my heart and worked on me. Even when I wasn't directly thinking about the book, stuff would occur to me. Most of what we do, we do automatically, like driving a car. Living in an intimate relationship is more complex than driving a car and there's more at stake, but it's still run mainly by reflexes and habits. This book challenged mine and changed them.

A lot of the discoveries weren't that new. You know how that is. Sometimes you can watch someone do something that you already knew how to do, except they do it better, without all those extra moves. It's happened with me in social dancing and playing music and doing public speaking and counseling. There are those moments when I go, "Wow! Cool! I didn't know that was possible!" Watching mastery gives me permission to get creative, to try something new. That happened with this project. That's been exciting and maybe the biggest gift of the whole project, but I still feel I need to be more specific and more vulnerable. Be gentle with me. I'm about to list many things I've needed to learn in order to be a better person.

I Learned More About How Saying "No" Is A Generous Act.

The relationship most immediately affected by the creation of this book was my relationship with Marilyn, my collaborator. We learned to argue productively. There were times when she would put forward her vision of what we had to do and all I could know in my mind was that I didn't agree. She's quite verbal and I'm quite committed to being a good listener. I would lose my connection with my own thinking while I was trying to understand her ideas.

Well, okay. It is difficult to hold two contradictory ideas in mind at the same time. And it was often tempting to just agree, especially for me because I have a wussy side to my character. But I cared so much about what we were doing and wanted it to reflect both our best intuitions.

So I had to take stands. This was a challenge for me. For one thing, sometimes I had to listen and understand and disagree without having a counter proposal. Sometimes it would take me days before I could find my own vision. She figured that out before I did that that was how I worked. Often she told me to take some time by myself before our next work session. (It's funny that she had a similar struggle, but I'm just talking about my stuff right now.)

All this had a paradoxical result. My willingness to say "no" made me more agreeable. When I did agree, I agreed more deeply. When I didn't agree, I still didn't get upset, not even a little. That's been a great benefit to me.

I also could see how my willingness to disagree has become the test of whether a relationship is meaningful. My comfort in disagreeing is a measure of a relationship's solidity.

I'm Still Learning How, As A Man, To Be Ever More Grateful For The Presence In My Life Of "Women Of Valor."

I was thinking about how the men here appreciated their wives and then I learned that there is a song that many observant Jewish men sing every Sabbath and it's in praise of their wives. (I've never been a very observant Jew.) The song is called *Eshet Chayil* and it means "Women of Valor." The mythology is that Abraham sang it about Sarah, his wife.

Eshet Chayil is a song of gratitude sung by men to honor a wife of great character. How wonderful for her husband to have complete confidence in her, how beautifully she masters practical things, how generous and caring she is, astute and wise. "Charm is deceptive," says the song, "Beauty is fleeting, but a woman of valor has great character and is due all honor that a man can give her."

This is a sentiment I saw over and over in these interviews. These folks appreciated their spouses. They trusted what their spouses saw in them, strengths and not-so-strengths.

Just spending time absorbing these sentiments of honor and appreciation challenged me. Yes I am in great awe of certain women, their strengths, their character, their heart, and their mind. (A moment's pause in honor of my mother.) I also saw how I am like Ronnie, how in awe I am of the practicality of women. At the same time, I was surprised to find in myself a certain small-minded vein of competitiveness between yours truly. and some of the great women in my life.

It's difficult to admit this, but to rein it in I have to. I often think about Haim saying "I was wild and she tamed me," and then, after a bit, Caroline added, "It was like dropping water on a stone." In other words, she did it through softness, clarity and persistence. Lucky Man. I take courage and inspiration from that exchange.

Later I learned that, according to some Kabbalistic teachings, only the men needed to be re-incarnated to correct the mistakes they'd made in their previous lives. Whatever mistakes women make during any particular lifetime, these are corrected in heaven. For them, reincarnation is an act of generosity. A woman only comes back in order to help her soul mate become a better person. If men are the ones who do the studying and discussing, it's because they are the ones who need to learn. Women just "know."

I don't accept that completely, but it's tempting and worth thinking about. Haim said, of Caroline, "Even when she's wrong, she's right."

I Have Some Of The Same Fears And Mixed Feelings About Lilith That Many Men Do.

I had to think a lot about Lilith. Lilith is an archetype, a character in a story who is much less complex than an actual person.

She gives us a way to think about a certain dimension of the female psyche. A woman who is very "Lilith," is a woman who is very powerful and very sexual. An interesting example of a Lilith is Carmen, from the opera. She sang, "Si je t'aime, prends garde toi," or, in English, "If I love you, you better watch out."

I understand the warning. Lilith has been a challenge for many men, me among them. Ohad was a man who welcomed that challenge. I felt he was telling me, "Hey, this is fabulous and thrilling. Don't let your fear chase you away. Step up."

At some level I am both fascinated by, and a fan of, that Lilith power when I see it in my partner. I counsel men and for many men, this is a challenge that they do not want to acknowledge or respect. "Me? Afraid of a woman?" A lot of those guys have to learn the hard way and many never learn.

After these interviews, I see more clearly where that fear of Lilith lurks in my own heart. The fact that I see it in myself has made it possible for me to have some pretty interesting conversations with some of those guys. It's also made it possible for me to open up more fully to the Lilith in my own life.

There Really Are Limits to Intimacy.

In any relationship, no matter how close, it is still important for partners to appreciate how they are still, nonetheless, two separate people. Shefa and Rachmiel emphasized this and so did Leibish and Deena. Even Ronnie and Karen talked about how we have to respect what is open and what is not. For myself, there are times when I need to step away just so I can know my own mind.

Inevitably we each will have our own moods, our own fears and joys and these are not the responsibility of our partner. Inevitably there are parts of my inner most soul that my partner cannot easily know, understand or share.

One of the more paradoxical places I am reminded of how there is a separation within the togetherness is in lovemaking.

In sexual union a simultaneous orgasm is not always necessary and the search for one can spoil the experience couples share together. When she says, "Oh, God," I'm happy for her even if it's not an "Oh God" moment for me. We do have to give each other our moments.

One of the more surprising places I was able to apply the idea that my primary relationship is with God and that others then get the overflow was in my guitar playing. I have always been struck by how distracted I can be when others are listening. It's so difficult to maintain my relationship to the beauty of the music when I am tempted to play more for the other person than I am playing for myself. Not enough differentiation. My meditation, my communication with Source, or God, whatever you call it, or "my inner Self," I need that. I cannot ask my partner to provide that. But that's the theory. Practice is another matter. I need constant reminders, even now, at my advanced age.

There Were Things About My Way Of Loving That Are Rather Uniquely Mine And That's A Good Thing.

There is an old Jewish teaching: When the time comes for God to judge me for my life, He will not say, "Why were you not more like Moses?" He will say, "Why were you not more like Philip?" The same idea came up in a survey someone did of people's last wishes, or regrets. One of the most common last wishes was this one: I wish I had been more like who I really am. So it's obvious to me that I am not the only one who acquired the habit of measuring myself against others.

And yet here I am doing this book and thinking about how I'd like to be more poetic like Rabbi Ronnie Cahana, or more of a teacher like Rabbi Yisroel, more of a story teller like Andrea, and on and on. And then at some point I remembered something my son said to me one time. He was talking about movie actors. "There are so many ways of being awesome." The more we are able to appreciate all those different ways of being awesome, the more easily we can find our own unique way of doing a great job.

In the introduction we asked the question, "Why is this couple not like any other couple." As we went through the interviews it became clear how each of these couples was successful in very distinctly different ways. We need courage to be awesome in our own very particular way.

Silences Say More than Words.

Some silences are like the calm before a storm, or pause before a cry of pain.

On the other hand there are those silences in the wilderness, or those at four in the morning, very full, evocative and nurturing.

Under the busyness one can find what Joseph Campbell once called, "the Word underneath the words." Sometimes this Word beneath the words is apparent in a kiss. Sometimes it's present in bed when you snuggle like spoons, when that very specific and essential melody of that other person fills your mind. Campbell said, "The best things cannot be told, the second best are often misunderstood. After that comes civilized conversation."

These folks seemed to cultivate those silences. Charles and Laura talked about them explicitly. So did Yisroel and Sara.

Our Genesis and Exodus Stories Need to Be Told and Retold.

We have a whole organ in our brain devoted to creating and revising the story of our life and the stories of our relationships. We are creatures who tell stories. If we don't re-tell the story, it's as if the story was lived in vain. Much of our spirituality is involved in the story we create.

In my Master's Thesis, I had written about the story that two people spontaneously create and cherish when they become a couple. Spontaneously. That's important. Some part of our soul grabs this story and holds it as a metaphor of the promise and souvenir of the challenge of that relationship, a souvenir of why it matters. It's worth saying those stories out loud from time to time. In this book we are calling those stories "Genesis" stories.

One of the surprises for me in creating this book was that several people also had Exodus stories. Exodus stories are a private and personal version of a moment when the relationship shifts and with it, the spiritual path of the couple. Laura talked about that moment alone in the coffee shop when she realized that she received unconditional love from Charles and that God gave her that, too. And Victor talked about that moment in the living room with Nadya when he recognized that he really did love her. Shefa had her story of the vision of Eliahu telling her that she could change her life.

I think we all have such stories, our personal epiphanies. Sometimes the moments are very small but it's worth honoring them.

I Still Have Not Sufficiently Appreciated How Much Personal Success Must Include Benefiting Others.

In the community where I grew up, for many other people, "achieving your highest potential," meant getting richer, more powerful, more respected and more famous. Charles also talked about that. What were we supposed to do with our lives? Be a doctor. Marry a doctor. Win the Game. Win the Case. Get the Promotion. Trade Up. Be the Best. I do not remember being exhorted to "Do something that benefits others." (Yisroel's advice to the young woman who wanted to find a husband.) So maybe being a "do-gooder" is not given enough respect in certain quarters.

In these interviews we were always in conversation with people who had deliberately embraced higher goals than just being right, being loved, being sexually fulfilled, being admired or being feared. These folks we interviewed helped others, they taught, they served. They were basically givers.

When I first heard about Shefa and Rachmiel's kissing meditation, sending their love out to bless the world, or Ohad and Dawn making their lovemaking into a prayer for the world, I thought it was cute and erotic. It took a while for the deeper message to sink in, this idea that everything one does needs to be seen in a larger perspective. We can always be serving something bigger than ourselves.

Somehow hearing these people talk about their lives made me more invested in making this book as good as I could. I have no idea whether anyone beyond a circle of friends will read it. Even so, I am so clear that neither money nor fame are primary motivations. I want it to be something others will benefit from, as I have.

So Is A Love Relationship Like A Messiah?

That was the idea that I shared with Marilyn, the idea that launched this project. So what did I finally think?

In these interviews, did we see folks willing to reshape their deepest habits so that their relationship would be a happier place for them and their partner? Yes. That's what I saw. Over and over I saw these folks giving thought to who they were together and how they were together. They spoke about their partnership knowingly. He's like this and I'm like that and this is how we are together. To see things in these dimensions is a deep perception. One of my favorite moments was when Karen gestured to the space between her and Ronnie and said, "This is home."

But it wasn't just about knowledge and comfort. Their relationship was where they practiced the best things they knew about love. What they did was a kind of service. They did it for their partner and also for the partnership. What they did was personal and purposeful.

There is this Jewish tradition of *Tikkun Olam,* (and in doing this book I became much more aware of it) and it means "healing the world." The acts we do have the purpose of making the world a better place in which to live. If that isn't done at "home," as Karen called it, then how real can it be?

To me, the relationship between marital love and spirituality seemed very chicken-and-egg. The commitment to making the world a better place surely must include what happens at home and that was one of the realizations for Haim and Caroline.

At the same time, the commitment to making their love nest a real nest of love must also spread outward into the world. This would be Lisa's and Andrea's rock-in-the-pond.

It seemed to me that the love they had for their partner and their relationship put everything else into perspective. Each menial act, like making a brick (or a meal for someone) and each medium act, like building a wall (or developing a career) was best understood as part of building a temple (creating a relationship that shines love into the world.) In this way the relationship became a source of transformation.

So even though Shefa and Rachmiel put an important nuance on our thesis when they said their primary relationship was with "Source" or God, and that the overflow goes to their partner, I still feel comfortable with my original belief. A loving relationship with another human being, because it's where our most intimate self is on the line, is the primary agent of transformation. Shefa says that their relationship is the "measure" of their spirituality.

Am I Revealing Too Much By Talking About What I Needed To Learn?

I said that there was safety in the "we" voice and I'm leaving that safety to write this closing essay. I made a deliberate decision to be vulnerable. For me, part of learning something new is admitting that I didn't know it before. It was so easy to see myself as being like Victor when he admitted that he was a guy who liked to score "debating points" and he had to stop doing that in order to learn a thing or two from Nadya. In this essay I've tried to admit where I've had to rein myself in. I've done that to solidify my learning.

Does that mean that there is some relationship between vulnerability and spiritual transformation? This question takes me back to the Bible story of Jacob wrestling with the angel. He was transformed spiritually and re-named. The cost to him was that for the rest of his life he walked with a limp. Walking with a limp is an interesting metaphor for a man who was so wily and clever. These folks were willing to reveal what they didn't know and had to learn. And they were willing to do it as a service, so folks like me could learn from their struggles. Amazing.

There were couples we spoke to who either refused our request for an interview or backed out later. I can certainly sympathize.

It makes me understand even more clearly the courage and generosity of those who decided to contribute.

There is Always More to be Seen and Told

Just as I have worked and re-worked my understanding of whatever this book is about, I think we all rework our personal stories. It's possible that our spiritual work is to tell and retell our stories until we arrive at a version we can live with and die with.

Working as a psychologist I often notice how, with unhappy couples, their story gets reduced to one or two talking points. Their view of each other is correspondingly narrowed and they see less of each other. When a relationship is a source of personal transformation, partners see more and there are always more possibilities. Their story is always unfolding. These couples seemed aware of that, that there were many chapters in their story, and that they were somewhere in the middle of it.

I go back to that young student under the bed seeking a peek into what happened when his wise older teacher and his wife made love. At first I thought it was just a story about spying on the physical act of lovemaking. But there had to be so much more going on.

Think about that incredible sharing from Haim and Caroline about what happens between them late at night in bed when the rest of the house is asleep. They talked, they told each other stories about their day. It made me think that when two who have been together a long time do make love, everything between them is present, the good, the bad, everything.

I was grateful to Reb Leibish for his story about the student who hid himself under his Rabbi's bed. Originally, I thought his point was that the teaching was included in the Talmud as a *story*. But then I remembered that it had been Leibish's wife, Deena, who told him to tell us that story. That changed the context of the story for me. It was a story she wanted him to tell.

What were they trying to get us to see? The story, obviously, went to the very heart of our project and became, in some sense, one of our central metaphors. Here I am, that young man who hid himself, coming back to share what I have learned.

What would I, as that young student, have said to my wife later that night when I got home? And what would she have said to me?

I don't think I would have told her before I did it what I was planning to do. I have too much respect for her authority and I would have been worried that she'd try to talk me out of it. Would she have wanted to join me? That's impossible. This particular curiosity is definitely a guy thing, I think. I bet she would have had a special sympathy for the Rabbi's wife. Imagine one of her husband's students hiding under her marital bed.

What if that young man didn't say anything? What if he went home, made love to his wife with a passion he'd never revealed before? Would she wonder what made him change? Would she ask?

I'm so grateful that we heard from the spouses in this book. I'm so grateful that I had a wise female collaborator. The Talmud is a record of many conversations among men.

Is there some lack of female perspective in all this? There are many thoughts there about how to be a good husband. Wouldn't you think that the rabbis' wives had many conversations on this same topic?

What did the women talk about in the moist social privacy of a ritual bath? What did they share about their marital intimacies before drying off, getting dressed, putting on their scarves and going home to make love to their husbands?

Did they ever tell their husbands? I suspect many of them did. But then they were already mature women.

Is it possible that the young student would have learned all he needed to know by listening to his wife?

On the other hand, possibly he, a young man, needed moral support from the older and wiser men in his small community to do whatever his wife would have dared to ask for, if she dared speak, if he had dared to speak of these things. Perhaps it was easier to hide under his Rabbi's bed than talk to his wife about their lovemaking? Maybe this too is a teaching point.

My heart goes out to this brave young man and his implied wife in the Talmud story. Let's wish them the best. Let's assume he came home, told the story, and she suppressed her laughter, or didn't, or was charmed by his youthful earnestness, or by his audacious ways, and that gave them both an additional thrill, or a laugh, in their happy sexual times together.

When I was a young boy there was one man I studied carefully so I could learn how that man acted in love and that man was not an austere Rabbi.

That man was my father. He and mom had a fierce love between them but it had some strange secrets. I still remember the time I woke up and heard through the wall an argument from their bedroom, my mom's muffled accusatory tone and my father's conciliatory tone. I was maybe five. I didn't want them angry at each other. I remember another time, when I was older, maybe ten, and I heard the low rumble of his voice coming through the walls and my mother's laughter. Why and how they loved each other was, for me, one of life's most fascinating mysteries. No wonder I went for a doctorate in relationship psychology.

There Was More.

There was so much wisdom here but I have to stop somewhere. I'm sure you readers will have seen things I didn't see. Certainly Marilyn and I had different perspectives and sensibilities. I came to know my own mind in the context of those fruitful conversations with my compatible and wise collaborator. I can't emphasize this enough.

But now I will stop and let Marilyn have the microphone.

And... from Marilyn Bronstein

Under the Bed, What Did I Learn?

I will answer the question with another question. (It's a Jewish thing.) What was I even doing under the bed? What did I hope to learn?

What intrigued me the most about the story was not what happened while the student was under the bed, nor what happened after he went home, but the last line, when he said, "This Torah, too, we need to learn." Certainly the first lesson I learned under the bed is that so much depends on WHO is under the bed and WHY they are there and WHAT they need to know.

So let me just clarify why I was there. I, personally, was always a believer when it came to love. I wanted to inspire others, to remind them that love is possible and that love can be a transformative experience. I wanted to collect the evidence.

What I didn't realize is that the experience of observing "under the bed" together can be almost as intimate as sharing a bed together. And as transformative.

I began to realize that my collaborative project with Philip involved more than just an exploration of what happens when couples live and love together. It was an exploration of collaboration itself. We were learning about the inevitable tension between keeping your own voice, while still making room for the other's. How does anyone do that with integrity and love?

I didn't expect to experience that challenge so intensely in myself and witness it so clearly in my collaborator. Ultimately I learned about relationships through doing relationship. There really is no other way.

At the beginning of the project I thought we should have two separate voices. I kept insisting that we needed separate chapters in each of our voices, and then I retreated to just asking for separate paragraphs. Then, somehow, it became both of us discussing each interview and that conversation evolved into just those "blue thread" commentaries, one per interview, hours of passionate, heated discussions about what we felt was the essence of each story summarized in a few paragraphs.

Philip wrote the first drafts. Then we discussed and revised until we could agree on a voice that clearly represented both our points of view. I was amazed at myself. How strongly I would argue my points all through this collaboration! I had always prided myself on being a person who aimed to please, so easy to get along with, so laissez-faire. Yet there I was, arguing over a comma, totally standing my ground. I was learning when to push for my point of view, when to relinquish it, and when to say, "Okay, maybe we are both wrong, let's try something else entirely that we can both agree on."

Our way of collaborating evolved. The first interviews were all in one voice. Then, at a certain point on our journey, maybe after the 7th interview, it was clear that one voice wasn't going to be adequate.

Philip said, "Maybe we should speak in two voices, not one," and that felt really right to me. In a way it was always what I had hoped for, but I guess our relationship needed time and experience to be ready for such risky business. It was a very interesting process.

So now that this project is almost over, I realized, both by listening to the stories of how these nine beautiful couples all do love, each in their own individual way, and also by negotiating with Philip, my collaborator, every step of the way, that *this* is the Torah I was there to learn: If it's a good relationship, there has to be room for both of us.

Love means never having to always agree.

Now that I am being asked to express myself on my own (without my ghost collaborator), I find myself feeling like the Little Mermaid who has lost her vocal chords. I had been expending so much energy trying to work with someone else, to let go of working on my own, that now when I am called to offer my own thoughts in my own words, I am struggling to know what I want to say.

All that being said, what did I learn?

Love and Marriage really can go together.

Like the song says, "Love and marriage…like a horse and carriage."

I have been carrying on a long-distance romance for 19 years. I'm totally in love with this man. So I always knew that love was possible, but I was not so sure about love and co-habitation.

All the couples we interviewed lived together. I'd never done that successfully. It was inspiring to see these relationships close up, all the wrinkles showing, and also all the beauty. It seemed that the wrinkles only enhanced the beauty. The couples did not gloss over the tough spots but embraced them as endearing and were almost grateful for them because they taught them so much. So it is possible, you can live together, it can be very good. Not that we're moving in together anytime soon, but still, it's nice to know.

Embracing Imperfection

I am actually a closet perfectionist. I keep waiting till I get it right before I come out, so I was very moved by the acceptance, and forgiveness of each other's foibles and idiosyncrasies I saw in each interview. They cherished the imperfection of each other and themselves. I learned from them that you really don't need to be enlightened or perfect to live with someone.

Laura and Charles were so amused and forgiving of themselves and each other's little imperfections. Everyone will make mistakes and that's ok. As Shefa and Rachmiel said, we will always try to make new mistakes.

A sense of humor helps. There should be an addendum to the serenity prayer, "G-d grant me the ability to be able to laugh at the things I cannot change or control." I think Rabbis are by nature great storytellers and a large part of the telling is in the humor.

And it seems that no matter what is going wrong in their lives; Rabbis are able to delight in it on some level, because they know they can use it as fodder for a great story, maybe in *shul* the next day.

Balancing the Me and the We

Rabbi Hillel said, *"If I am not for myself who will be for me. Yet if I am for myself alone what good am I? And if not now when?"*

In theory it is easy. In practice, how do you do these two things simultaneously? Again and again in a love relationship, or a collaboration, the question comes up, "Who is going to lead and who will follow now, at this moment?" How do you decide?

In his relationship classes Yisroel talks about how one must set aside one's own needs, what he calls needing to have the vessel in order to receive the blessing. He's advocating giving and serving. On the other hand Caroline insists that it is a gift to put demands on your partner so he can meet your needs. Asking him to keep you more satisfied helps him grow. This is her teaching to women who come to her seeking relationship advice. So which is it?

Both teachings are true. In any relationship you have to figure out the balance. How much of yourself do you want to hang on to and how much do you want to compromise? The same question comes up over and over. All the couples we interviewed had interesting things to teach about the challenge of finding this balance.

Overall, the guiding principle that worked was the idea that it wasn't just about "me" or "you," it was about Something Bigger. This shifted their perspective.

What did the relationship require at that moment? Because they were committed to a spiritual discipline they were practiced in giving themselves over to a higher power. This allowed them to more easily forego their own needs for the sake of the relationship.

Lisa and Andrea talked about how they were a team and how, although they each had their portfolios, they were both willing to do whatever it took to make their lives run more smoothly. They explained that ultimately it is not about them; it is about how they can serve others.

What particularly impressed me about their story is that because they were both of the same gender they didn't have societal expectations as to who should be doing what in the relationship. They had to create their own systems for dividing management responsibility. As Andrea put it, *"I take care of vomit, she takes care of blood."*

I had the impression that all of the Rabbis we spoke to, who, after all, belong to a profession that has a lot of power and prestige attached to it, have learned to hang on to their humility this way, by always considering their relationship and it's needs. Perhaps this practice reminds them that it is a higher power that is guiding them to lead their flock. They are only the vessel.

Also, sometimes the partners of the Rabbis had to learn to put limits on their partners. Many of them talked about it in terms of the balance between *Gevurah* (boundaries and justice) and *Chesed* (overflowing generosity and loving-kindness). Rabbis seem to be particularly susceptible to overdoing it on the *Chesed* side, showering overflowing love on EVERYONE regardless of the situation.

Their partners seem to be the ones that need to remind them that saying NO is sometimes more loving than saying YES. (Maybe that's what the biblical Abraham, the symbol of pure *Chesed*, had to learn when asked to sacrifice his son, but I shall restrict myself and not go off on a Bible teaching mission now).

In Praise of Structure

Never in a million years would have I guessed that I would be defending structure.

But I came to understand that structure was one of the secrets of how these relationships survived and flourished. Each of these couples lives a complicated life with a lot of external demands. Each of these couples has found a structure in Judaism that holds their relationship together and binds them. They all have a daily practice, a weekly rhythm, a lunar cycle, and a yearly cycle.

One of the most valuable things I learned, is that whether one is religious or not, these rituals of quality-time, the practice of setting aside time either to be together consciously or to consciously be apart, can bring a relationship back into alignment. Without such structures, a relationship can spin out of control or die a slow death.

I think every single couple mentioned Shabbas. Ronnie and Karen talked how every Shabbas they rediscover each other again. It's that quiet intimate time together. Several other couples said that, since they "work" on Shabbas they make "dates" to make sure they still get that time together.

Other couples, Shefa and Rachmiel and Deena and Leibish, stressed the importance of "time out," when they each have a chance to disconnect and find their individual voices again. And then they come back to their partner centered and ready to relate to the essence of each other. Ohad and Dawn were probably the most extreme example of "time-apart." They consciously and openly took time to be with other partners, with the full understanding that they would always be returning to each other, their primary partner. But although they are *a little over the border for most people* (as they both acknowledge), still, the basic idea, to consciously taking time out and then, in a renewed state, to come back together, was a common practice among many of the couples.

For me, because of my long-distance relationship, finding time apart is what I do naturally. Listening to these couples made me realize that I, in my life, needed to set aside more quality time with my partner.

Commitment: Persistence

"That's it! I call it quits, this is never going to work!"

It is not obvious when it is appropriate to say this and when it is better to slog through the tough stuff so you come out on the other side, stronger and yet more able to share your vulnerabilities.

The couples we interviewed all had staying power. Not that everything was always smooth between these couples. Au contraire. But they had the tools to get back to each other again when they were slipping away. Laura expressed this when she said that after 20 years of marriage she had come to understand that *"God is always there for you."* She had come to this understanding because Charles was always there for her. No matter what happened, their cardinal rule was – You don't leave. You stay. You work it out.

And more. You don't just stay, you really put in the effort to get to know each other and get to know yourself. Staying means being prepared to not know what to do next. It means putting yourself in a position where you have to learn something.

These couples are mystics; they know they don't know. Their exploration of their partner and themselves is never-ending, there is always something new to discover, there is always another place to go together. After 36 years of being together Ronnie still talks about discovering the mysteries of his mate.

Commitment II: Patience

They understood patience and what it means to wait for their partner to understand what they see already. So many of them referred to this. Deena talks about waiting for Leibish to realize what she already knew. Shefa also talks about this. Andrea also. And of course Nadya too who instantly "saw" they would be lifetime partners. Months later, Victor was still clueless about who Nadya was; he had to go to her birthday party to find out what she looked like. And Haim talks about how long it took for Caroline to tame him.

These couples also knew how to wait until the time *is ripe*. Haim and Caroline told us about touching feet under the table at Shabbas while they have all these guests over. Dawn and Ohad described almost the same scene of gazing into each other's eyes intimately at the table with everyone else sitting there maybe half aware of what was going on.

A moment or two of intimacy in the privacy of their own room or maybe even in a public setting, those few stolen moments, seemed to sustain them through the times they cannot be together.

The persistence, and the patience, and the ability to wait for the good things, forfeiting instant gratification; all this is commitment.

Diversity

Like Haim says 'If you are identical, two is one too many.' Yet how different can you be from your partner and still be able to live with them, and also be "happily ever after"?

Diversity seemed to be fundamentally important to these people. I noticed that in many of their Genesis stories, one of the partners would be struck by some particular attribute of their partner that they found off-putting and yet also attractive. They all seemed to play with this tension of how different do you want your partner to be from you. You can see this in every couple.

What was so interesting is that in all their Genesis stories they saw the differences immediately. Nonetheless, they consciously choose to take on the challenge of living together and loving together. So it's either in spite of those differences or because of them, or both. Through dealing with their differences they each became stronger. Each reclaimed a part of himself, herself, that was dormant or suppressed before they encountered each other. And their bond as a couple became stronger.

That was also true for my collaboration with Philip. I was constantly surprised and struck by how differently the stories landed on our ears; same stories but you would never know it because we heard them so differently. After a while I began to wonder.

Maybe we'd been under the bed on different nights. As we worked together our differences became more and more evident. Sometime only after months of discussion did we discover that we had totally different understandings of what the couple was trying to communicate.

Also it was fascinating to hear the couples themselves tell different renditions of a shared story. It is amazing how gender and genes and different sensibilities cause the same story to be told so differently.

We all live in our stories. To truly set aside one's own conditioning and try to really hear the other's story, I think that is the challenge. The wider the differences between you and your partner or collaborator, the bigger the potential for misunderstanding on the one hand but also the bigger the opportunity there is for widening your horizons and coming to understand something in a totally new way. You need to decide how much risk you can tolerate; the bigger the risk the more the potential for bigger rewards.

Modeling

When we asked Ronnie how he knew so much about love when he was young he said that he watched his parents' marriage and he wanted a love like that. We do need models. For Shefa and Rachmiel it was to have a love like the lovers in Song of Songs. Rachmiel said, *"I would ask myself, is that the way they would speak to each other in Song of Songs, if not, then I don't want to speak like that either."* Victor and Nadya held up the model "One Soul", how the two can become one.

As I remarked at the beginning of this book, the old rules about relationships are not necessarily applicable to the majority of people today. What I saw in these couples was an ability to hold on to a vision, a model of what they wanted to aspire to in their relationship. This gave their relationship a compass, a direction and it did more. By having their own vision of their relationship they could also let their relationship be a model for others.

Some, like Deena and Leibish, take an old model and improve upon it. They follow very closely the wisdom of the Talmud and Torah and its laws and this became the blueprint for their relationship.

And yet they also take it to another level incorporating the modern world into that old blueprint. Inadequate models can be as useful as positive ones if they lead you to create a better one.

Ohad and Dawn use the story of Lilith and Adam as a cautionary tale as to how things can go wrong. They use this myth as an impetus to re-balance the inequality between the sexes but also allowing their expressive, maybe more primitive, creative, natural sides to come forward.

Not only do we need models, we also are models for others. Yisroel and Sara, Haim and Caroline, Nadya and Victor, Ohad and Dawn all hold classes teaching others how to have a fulfilling relationship.

Laura and Charles model a loving family for their community. Laura assures her community that, like a loving family, they can hold differences, and this will not split them apart.

Lisa and Andrea. They talk about how to model relationships that are free from the usual gender type-casting. The model they use, if any, is maybe the New York Yankees where each person on the team does whatever is necessary to make the team function optimally. They see themselves as a "rock in the pond" using their own relationship to influence the world around them.

All of them are public figures and certainly must be conscious that the rest of the community looks to them for how to "make love". As we have seen there are so many different ways to do it, even when we are restricting our observations to Rabbis and their partners.

We all learn from each other.

Unconditional Love with Conditions

After 20 years of marriage, Laura discovered that there were limits, lines that could not be crossed in their relationship even though they were never, ever named. That made me realize something. Even unconditional love comes with conditions.

This helps me understand in a new way the ceremony that Ronnie talked about, the ceremony before you get married of "The Conditions," the *T'naim*. I now understand the need, and the responsibility, for each partner to spell out the specific conditions under which each one's Love will flourish and grow. Love needs a safe, secure container.

Today many couples write their own personal wedding vows. This is their way of stating conditions. Two people are vowing that they will remain together "forever" as long as these conditions are in place.

ome couples revisit, renew, or revise, their vows every year. When someone understands that maybe these conditions were not accurate or adequate, then it is time to renegotiate.

Love is a Generator

At first I thought *"How you get the love you want,"* or even *"How you enrich your love"* was the big question. I was surprised. Without being prompted all the couples talked about how they use their love to inform and transform their community.

Love, for these couples, was not the end point; it is a means to a higher end. Love is a generator. It can make good happen in the world.

So many of them talked about this. Shefa and Rachmiel, Ohad and Dawn, Victor and Nadya, Lisa and Andrea, Ronnie and Karen talked about the importance of teaching your children about Love and how to take it out into the world.

Although I didn't fully understand this when we began this project, I realize now that I intuitively understood something about the *Moshiach;* the *Moshiach* wants to bring peace and love to the world. To teach that you must live it. Maybe not necessarily as a couple, but in some way, you need to test out your belief systems in an organic way, in a relationship where your needs and wants and ideas bump up against someone else's.

Of course when you do figure out how to navigate these differences you want to share it with others. But it is more than just sharing a technique. You want to share your delight, your gratitude, and your pleasure with others. A smile can change someone's day. Someone else's calm can calm you down.

We all are rocks in the pond whether we are conscious about it or not. This is the *Moshiach* concept, that how we live our lives can profoundly affect the world around us and that if we are so lucky to receive love, then take that love and let it flow to others around us, to enrich their lives too.

Tachlis (the bottom line)

It's funny. I have been on a journey with Philip, exploring the notion of relationship as spiritual path through my own experience but also through his ears and eyes and through the stories of the nine couples.

When you set out on a journey with someone to create something together, whether it be a love relationship or a book, or something else, in one sense you know where you are going, but in another, when you get there you realize you had no idea.

My ex, after we split up, chided me, saying, "You used me, you grew from this relationship and I never did!" I have come to realize that any intimate relationship, whether it be a love relationship or a collaboration, will stretch and challenge you. It will help you to grow *IF* you allow it to. It requires a certain amount of humility, a certain amount of confidence in yourself and your partner and in life itself, maybe G-D, or the creative process or something inexplicable that goes beyond what you can knowingly control.

It also requires staying power, a commitment that you will not leave when things are not going your way, or you don't feel you are being heard or understood. It becomes the lab where your belief systems and moral standards and ideas about yourself and the world around you get tested. This is where you really learn: by doing, not by thinking, and by observing how someone other than yourself does things, and by being open to new perspectives.

Rabbi Gafni once said at a wedding I attended, "When two people are willing to stand under the *chuppah* (wedding canopy) together in front of a whole community and declare their vows to each other, they are saying that they believe that everything is possible and when they do this, they take the whole community up with them. At least for that moment everyone believes that everything is possible".

A wedding is not only for the good of the couple it is for the good of the whole community. It inspires us all; it renews our hopes. If that is what happens at the moment of marriage, how much more so for a couple that is still in love seven years, 20 years, 40 years after they have taken their nuptial vows? How much more can we be inspired by a couple that has lived together, gone through challenges together, and who still hold each other with so much gentleness, passion and respect?

So I guess my prayer of wanting a Messiah couple that could show me how this was possible was answered ten fold – nine couples interviewed plus us. Thank you to all my Messianic couples who have shown me that it is possible. Thank you to my collaborator who always believed it was possible. It is all possible.

Epilogue

No Two People Make Love In The Same Way.

Or do anything else the same for that matter. As we look over the separate essays we wrote, we are both struck by how different our separate voices are. And this is after we've spent thousands of hours working together. Clearly, we are unique and separate souls, just like everyone else.

We've spoken of the common themes in these interviews. But the most important similarity is that they are all different. Each couple is unique. And each individual in each couple is unique. This sort of personal authenticity is perhaps a mark of high spirituality. And this is perhaps the most important lesson.

Ultimately being under someone else's bed can take you only so far. Learning how others make love can be useful only if it inspires you, dares you, intrigues you, encourages you to go do something.

As Rabbi Hillel famously said, "Go forth and learn." Go forth. Make love. Do love. Explore love. Learn how to do it better and better.

About The Authors

Philip Alan Belove, M.A., Ed.D., is a public speaker, workshop leader and psychologist with M.A. from Alfred Adler Institute of Chicago, and Ed.D. from University of Massachusetts at Amherst. His focus is on how relationships work. His website is **www.drbelove.com**. As part of this focus he has explored and taught social dancing including swing and tango. He taught Communication between Men and Women at Keene State College for several years. He is a consulting psychologist with GBLA, a management consulting firm, and also maintains a private practice via internet and telephone. "Belov" is a common Russian name, like "Orlov" and "Chekov," and in Russian, it means "white." When the family arrived in America, the name was changed to "Belove," and thereby gained all those powerful connotations. Some people think the name on the website, Dr Belove, is a marketing ploy.

Marilyn Bronstein graduated from Maimonides College in Winnipeg where she studied with Rabbi Zalman Schachter-Shalomi as well as other great Rabbis that have inspired in her a life-long fascination with Jewish studies. She has been a professor at Champlain College for the last 27 years and has recently retired. Now she has time for her two passions: people's stories and Judaism and how the two intersect. She composes Jewish chants and liturgy; she loves improvising in all of the creative arts: dance, singing, theatre, watercolors. she animates community events exploring Judaism through the arts. For 25 years, she was one of the guiding forces of Havurat Har Kodesh, a renewal group that was constantly exploring how to make Judaism relevant to our lives today. This is her first book.

www.ingramcontent.com/pod-product-compliance
Lightning Source LLC
Chambersburg PA
CBHW070637160426
43194CB00009B/1485